The Silent Revolution

DOI: 10.1057/9781137373502

Other Palgrave Pivot titles

Mercedes Bunz: The Silent Revolution: How Digitalization Transforms Knowledge, Work, Journalism and Politics without Making Too Much Noise

Mark Bracher: Educating for Cosmopolitanism: Lessons from Cognitive Science and Literature

Carroll P. Kakel III: The Holocaust as Colonial Genocide: Hitler's 'Indian Wars' in the 'Wild East'

Laura Linker: Lucretian Thought in Late Stuart England: Debates about the Nature of the Soul

Nicholas Birns: Barbarian Memory: The Legacy of Early Medieval History in Early Modern Literature

Adam Graycar and Tim Prenzler: Understanding and Preventing Corruption

Michael J. Pisani: Consumption, Informal Markets, and the Underground Economy: Hispanic Consumption in South Texas

Joan Marques: Courage in the Twenty-First Century

Samuel Tobin: Portable Play in Everyday Life: The Nintendo DS

George P. Smith: Palliative Care and End-of-Life Decisions

Majia Holmer Nadesan: Fukushima and the Privatization of Risk

Ian I. Mitroff, Lindan B. Hill, and Can M. Alpaslan: Rethinking the Education Mess: A Systems Approach to Education Reform

G. Douglas Atkins: T.S. Eliot, Lancelot Andrewes, and the Word: Intersections of Literature and Christianity

Emmeline Taylor: Surveillance Schools: Security, Discipline and Control in Contemporary Education

Daniel J. Hill and Daniel Whistler: The Right to Wear Religious Symbols

Donald Kirk: Okinawa and Jeju: Bases of Discontent

Sara Hsu: Lessons in Sustainable Development from China & Taiwan

Paola Coletti: Evidence for Public Policy Design: How to Learn from Best Practices

Thomas Paul Bonfiglio: Why Is English Literature? Language and Letters for the Twenty-First Century

David D. Grafton, Joseph F. Duggan, and Jason Craige Harris (eds): Christian-Muslim Relations in the Anglican and Lutheran Communions

Anthony B. Pinn: What Has the Black Church to Do with Public Life?

Catherine Conybeare: The Laughter of Sarah: Biblical Exegesis, Feminist Theory, and the Laughter of Delight

Peter D. Blair: Congress's Own Think Tank: Learning from the Legacy of the Office of Technology Assessment (1973–1995)

Daniel Tröhler: Pestalozzi and the Educationalization of the World

Geraldine Vaughan: The 'Local' Irish in the West of Scotland, 1851–1921

Matthew Feldman: Ezra Pound's Fascist Propaganda, 1935–45

Albert N. Link and John T. Scott: Bending the Arc of Innovation: Public Support of R&D in Small, Entrepreneurial Firms

DOI: 10.1057/9781137373502

palgrave▸pivot

The Silent Revolution: How Digitalization Transforms Knowledge, Work, Journalism and Politics without Making Too Much Noise

Mercedes Bunz
Leuphana University, Germany

palgrave
macmillan

DOI: 10.1057/9781137373502

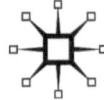

First published 2014 by
PALGRAVE MACMILLAN

Palgrave Macmillan in the UK is an imprint of Macmillan Publishers Limited, registered in England, company number 785998, of Houndmills, Basingstoke, Hampshire RG21 6XS.

Palgrave Macmillan in the US is a division of St Martin's Press LLC, 175 Fifth Avenue, New York, NY 10010.

Palgrave Macmillan is the global academic imprint of the above companies and has companies and representatives throughout the world.

Palgrave® and Macmillan® are registered trademarks in the United States, the United Kingdom, Europe and other countries.

ISBN: 978–1–137–37351–9   EPUB
ISBN: 978–1–137–37350–2   PDF
ISBN: 978–1–137–37349–6   Hardback

A catalogue record for this book is available from the British Library.

A catalog record for this book is available from the Library of Congress.

www.palgrave.com/pivot

DOI: 10.1057/9781137373502

Contents

DOI: 10.1057/9781137373502

Acknowledgements

When I started the endeavour of writing a book on digitalization, I sketched all the key words on a sheet of paper by drawing a tag cloud. Afraid that I had missed something important, I mailed the digital picture of my sketch to a friend for his opinion. He replied: 'It took me some time, but finally I found what is missing. The arrows!'

Of tremendous help when marking those arrows was my time as *The Guardian*'s technology reporter, but even more important was my encounter with the paper's editor Alan Rusbridger, whose inspiring interest in digitalization has always led the way much better than any navigation device would. Besides him, Alexander García Düttmann and Peter Hallward have been important role models who have inspired lateral thinking.

I have been able to use Matthew Fuller's and Geert Lovink's innovative ways of approaching digital media and have been inspired by Katherine Hayles's considerate, yet future-looking approach towards digitalization. On this occasion I would like to bow to Friedrich Kittler, who passed away while the book was being produced, and whose outstanding achievement in thinking media has deeply influenced me. I would like to thank the Centre for the Humanities and the Culture and Media Department of the University of Utrecht, which gave me the opportunity to write and discuss parts of the book as its Impakt Fellow, my editor Felicity Plester for her support and encouragement. Sascha Kösch, who had asked for the arrows, and Christian Heilbronn, my German editor at Suhrkamp, have devoted their time to bringing my thoughts into

DOI: 10.1057/9781137373502

shape as has my husband. I would like to thank my inspiring colleagues at the Hybrid Publishing Lab, Leuphana University, for dinners and discussions, especially Yuk Hui, Michael Dieter, and Marcus Burkhardt for helpfully knowing all the relevant publications in far greater detail than the British Library Catalogue or Google; Yuk has been an important adviser at large. My thanks also go to the anonymous peer reviewer for his or her very helpful suggestions, as well as to Ian Newby and Justin Jaeckle for their comments.

This book is dedicated to the British Library, a home for thoughts as much as for books. Its wide, airy reading rooms gave the endeavour of capturing digitalization enough room for such a weighty question to stretch, while its wobbly wireless internet connection left me with no choice but to face it. May our societies hold on to the importance of such places.

DOI: 10.1057/9781137373502

Preface

It is the surprising human response to the rise of the internet which started off this book. Maybe like some of my readers, I remember very well a time without it. Back then information was scarce, unlike today when it constantly follows us wherever we go, eager to be processed, day or night, like an annoying child that doesn't want to go to bed. Before the internet, it would take a lot of effort to find the right information. Whenever we wanted to know something, we had to ask a superior, or had to read two difficult books before we could find what we wanted to know in the third one. Or we simply couldn't find out. The tool that is today at our fingertips, the internet, has changed all of this. It patiently answers the simplest of questions. When was the last rocket launched from the Isle of Wight? What are the ingredients I need for Yorkshire pudding? What does skin cancer look like? In which Viennese street do I find the house that Wittgenstein helped building? What is discourse analysis? The internet provides some answers, most of them correct, some to be further verified.

But we weren't pleased. While some visionary geeks such as Katherine Hayles and Franco Moretti, Alan Liu and Matthew Fuller, Geert Lovink, Clay Shirky, or Cory Doctorow were analysing technology's new potential, the majority didn't share their fascination. The public wasn't delighted about the abundance of information; rather, it was concerned. This explains the wide echo of the question 'Is Google making us stupid?' posed in 2008 through the cultural critic Nicholas Carr's cover story on the monthly magazine *The Atlantic*. Within weeks, the question got

DOI: 10.1057/9781137373502

picked up by *The Observer*, the weekly magazine *Der Spiegel*, was written about in *The Wall Street Journal*, discussed on *BBC* websites, found on Dutch blogs, and in French magazines. One could say, it became a global concern. The medium provided human societies with information 24/7, and doing so it was internationally considered to make mankind stupid – a surprising and interesting response. There must be a reason for the response, which had better be understood.

I decided to look into it. Most people would agree that digitalization has been changing our societies as much as industrialization has, which had been invoked as a fascinating potential for our economy. However, the potential of digital technology seems to look different from a social point of view, where it has been mostly discussed as a threat. But isn't digital technology also an opportunity for our societies? Vast parts of our digitalization rely on royalty-free technology ever since in 1991 the World Wide Web was prototyped and tested at the French part of CERN, and as its British inventor Sir Tim Berners-Lee being part of the Opening Ceremony of London's Summer Olympic Games 2012 reminded the public by tweeting: 'This is for everyone.' A statement that should be taken very seriously, indeed. Digital communication is closely related to public space, more than ever as today 'it is largely by technology that contemporary society hangs together' (Franssen et al. 2010). Inspired by Hannah Arendt's *The Human Condition*, this book makes an effort to report some of the changes that we experience being with technology. In this respect, the book investigates digitalization by looking at the effects digital media has on Western societies. Like the philosopher Gilbert Simondon, I aim to show that technology is fundamentally related to us humans. In leaving any oppositional approach towards thinking 'being' behind, he, who has inspired my thinking the most, is as much a radical thinker as he is an outstanding philosopher of technology (more in Chapter 3). As in his book *Du mode d'existence des objets techniques*, most of my arguments root on technical examples.

Certainly, much like the machines in the past era, by now digital algorithms have affected almost every aspect of our lives, and unbalanced some of our cultural scales: algorithms have changed the way our societies are processing knowledge. The effect is that in today's expert societies, we all experience the transformation of our work. At the same time, algorithms have widely opened up access to the public sphere initializing new political opportunities soon to be fully discovered. Gathering some of our fierce debates on the effect of the digitalization

DOI: 10.1057/9781137373502

on knowledge, work, journalism, and politics, this book tries to get to the bottom of the issue, with the aim of exploring and comprehending these transformations better. In order to do this, the book describes the massive change and the new social options that come with it, starting with a historic comparison of our discussions of work and knowledge. The second part is directed at discussions of the public sphere and its digitalization captured through *thick* description. In terms of style this results in an unusual approach mixing the following two perspectives: a journalist's task that is to report the news, and a scholar's task that is to gather systematic knowledge. As this book reports the systematic change of knowledge and information by digitalization, it is situated between both perspectives. Thus, it is also a tentative endeavour in style, for which the writer begs forgiveness.

A second apology must be offered to computer scientists. In order to gather a better understanding of the role we humans play in the historic process, algorithms – effective procedures expressed as a finite list for calculating a function – will often not be looked upon in their informational sense. Chapter 1, for example, provides an overview of different theoretical approaches in the humanities, which discuss algorithms as the principle digitalization is built upon: computers, digital devices, software programs, internet platforms, apps, data sets, and search procedures, all these different areas are driven by them. Therefore algorithms exceed informatics thereby becoming a social technology that is massively transforming our society.

What social forces unfold with digitalization? To answer this question, this book is, of course, drawing on important academic research that has been undertaken in recent years. As media studies is by now a vast, rich, productive and much too lively discourse to be mapped, I only want to introduce the authors and institutions that informed this book with their research of the presence. Among those, the field of Software Studies critically evaluating computational processes to provide us with the necessary digital literacy has been important. In the nice and apt words of Matthew Fuller: 'algorithms are ways of thinking and doing that leak out of the domain of logic and into everyday life' (Fuller 2008, 1). As software becomes part of our world, it is shaping our societies. To explore this is the concern that is at the core of this book.

Fortunately, this isn't a concern of a voice in the wilderness anymore. By now, influential institutions ponder the use of the internet on a social scale. Among others, the Oxford Internet Institute, the Berkman Center

DOI: 10.1057/9781137373502

of Harvard University, the Centre for Internet and Society in Bangalore, and the Massachusetts Institute of Technology (MIT) have promoted excellent research and financed important projects. Surely, their emphasis differs – the Berkman Center puts the focus on law, the Oxford Internet Institute on social studies, the Bangalore Centre for Internet and Society takes a postcolonial perspective, and the MIT puts technology at the core of all of its activities devoted to advancing knowledge. Still it could be said that they share the same intent: to explore the impact of digital technology on society. The critical turn of this is to be found at the Institute of Network Cultures, University of Amsterdam, directed by Geert Lovink, and the Open Media Initiative led by Gary Hall at the University of Coventry, among other playful satellites.

Their critical focus on the social impact of digital technology is something I share, even though my aim here is somewhat narrower. I want to confine my research to look specifically at our discourse of technology, an intellectual endeavour that is (1) following the road of the digital humanities, which is about to enfold itself in theoretical arguments beyond the simple use of digital tools (Berry 2012; Lunenfeld et al. 2012); (2) assuming that in every society the discourse of a technology organizes to a certain extent how this technology is used; this research owes a lot to the discourse analyses of Michel Foucault. Exploring the technical discourse starts with setting aside the virtual/real divide, which is replaced by a *thick* description comprising present and classic debates, actual developments, new channels of distribution, digital methods (Rogers 2013), and historical comparisons. Studying the discourse accompanying the rise of digital technology in order to comprehend how these tectonic shifts affect our social structures, the hypothesis is that we will learn at least partly about the question that fundamentally informs this book: What social forces unfold with digitalization?

DOI: 10.1057/9781137373502

palgrave▸pivot

www.palgrave.com/pivot

1

When Algorithms Learned How to Write

Abstract: *This chapter contributes to discussions in sociology of media that critically debate the interaction of algorithms with our knowledge and brain. Following Nicholas Carr (2010) and Katherine Hayles (2012) who have discussed the effect of information overload on reading, this chapter looks into algorithms that started to write using the example of a sports report writing algorithm 'Stats Monkey'. To add to the debate, the chapter delivers an overview of actual definitions of algorithms in the humanities, including Media Theory, Software Studies, and Digital Humanities. Then it traces today's debate back to the problem of Artificial Intelligence and the misconception of a 'Ghost in the Machine' (Ryle 1949). Having refuted the ghost, technology emerges as a tool, which nothing but shifts the parameter of knowledge.*

Keywords: algorithms, artificial intelligence, digital humanities, digital knowledge, fact, truth

Mercedes Bunz. *The Silent Revolution: How Digitalization Transforms Knowledge, Work, Journalism and Politics Without Making Too Much Noise*. Basingstoke: Palgrave Macmillan, 2014. DOI: 10.1057/9781137373502.

Digitalization changes how we know, and we do not know enough about it. That algorithms have learnt how to write, for example, wasn't expected. Nobody anticipated it, and the report of a college baseball game wasn't anything to grab anybody's attention with anyhow. 'The robots are coming. Oh, they are here!' wrote David Carr of *The New York Times* on the issue, half a year after the algorithm Stats Monkey had covered a Northwestern Wildcat baseball game in Illinois. Here is the thing with innovations: When it is plain as the nose on your face that from now on we need to see the world with different eyes, everybody is in shock. But before innovations become annoyingly obtrusive, they are often already among us, and pass by unnoticed. In this way, groundbreaking inventions have taken place in back rooms such as garden sheds or US garages. There, the first Apple and Microsoft inventions have been built, as these have been the places where man and machine have combined forces. With algorithms it is different. When in March 1998 the search engine Google, for example, was tested at google.stanford.edu, it was a research project. Algorithms don't need a place, but come into being as a rough idea or university project to be immediately launched and tested online. In a way, they don't hide in back rooms, but in front of our eyes, and only when they change the world do they become apparent.

We have known for quite a while that algorithms do an outstanding job with calculations. We also got used to the fact that on the internet, they look up what we want to know. Finally, they also started to write, a moment that the French philosopher Jacques Derrida would have not let gone by unnoticed. But are they really writing? Let's have a look into the procedure in order to understand what its social effect could potentially be.

The sports report writing algorithm Stats Monkey combines for his texts two techniques: first, it looks up the scores that are published online; second it investigates the most important players and the course of the game by making use of an algorithmic decision tree; and third it puts the outcome into a journalistic text using pre-written templates such as 'Team X takes an early lead and never looks back' or 'Team Y tries to rally late, but doesn't make it'. One click, and a bone dry, yet informative sport report is ready, faster than any journalist could even type a sentence. It reads as follows:

> SOUTH BEND, Ind. – Tony Bucciferro put the Michigan State Spartans on his back Sunday and spurred them to a 3–0 win over the Notre Dame Fighting Irish (7–11) at Frank Eck Stadium. Bucciferro kept the Fighting Irish off the board during his nine innings of work for Michigan State

DOI: 10.1057/9781137373502

(12–4). He struck out five and allowed one walk and three hits. Senior Matt Grosso was not able to take advantage of a big opportunity for the Irish in the ninth inning (Bunz 2010, further texts also cited by Carr 2009).

While we may criticize the text's prosaic quality we can't argue away that a cultural technique is automated: story telling. Up till then it had been exclusively a human skill. Now the algorithm Stats Monkey marks another historical moment of a digitalization that transforms our world as fundamentally as once industrialization did. For computers, search engines, and with them algorithms have already stolen into our daily lives, and the latter can be compared to the inventions that changed sluggish cotton manufacturing into a rapid textile industry at the beginning of the industrial revolution. Of course, this also came as a surprise: 'Capitalism arrived unannounced,' as the political economist Karl Polanyi puts it (Polanyi 1944, 89). In 1733 the Englishman John Kay patented his invention of the 'Flying Shuttle', a device that allowed the weft to be passed through the threads much faster, with 'a speed that cannot be imagined' as a contemporary noted (Wadsworth and de Lacy Mann 1931, 470). The device doubled the productivity of the weavers. Their increasing demand for yarn was answered in 1764 with the invention of the multi-spool machine, the 'Spinning Jenny'. The machine enabled one worker to work eight spools or more simultaneously. From England, the industrial revolution was on its way. Can the program Stats Monkey be understood as the revenant of the Spinning Jenny? The Stats Monkey program makes apparent that digitalization has taken on a dramatic scale. Its influence in our lives started with the World Wide Web at the European Organization for Nuclear Research, CERN, where in 1990 the first prototype of the information managing system for sharing knowledge has been tested. While the machines of the industrial revolution have automated human *work*, the algorithms of the digital revolution assist human *knowledge*. However, in the age of skilled work this affects our jobs as the American economists Erik Brynjolfsson and Andrew McAfee have pointed out in their awakening book *Race against the Machine* (2011). And other than in the industrial revolution, this time the automation won't hit the low-pay sector. Today, armies of expensive lawyers can be replaced by cheaper software, when algorithms help analyse 1.5 million documents for less than $100,000 (Markoff 2011). Some of the well-paid bond traders and bankers of the financial service such as Morgan Stanley will soon be exchanged with computers. Its head of interesting rates at this time, Glenn Hadden, is reported to tell colleagues

DOI: 10.1057/9781137373502

that 'the trading floor of the future will surround a few traders with the hum of powerful machines' (Lucchetti and Brett 2012). Also the dream job of the middle class, journalism, is affected with the first sports report writing programs developed and working, a case which demonstrates the current dilemma.

Invented by Professor Kristian Hammond's students at the Northwestern University in Illinois, the Stats Monkey is the fruit of a collaboration of the Department of Computer Science and its Medill School of Journalism, and was developed as an answer to media diversification and the financial crisis that have both made traditional journalism struggle (Intelligent Information Laboratory 2010). As print media had to follow their readers onto the internet, they had to find new revenue streams. Local coverage is especially troubled financially, after classifieds had left traditional media to find a new home online. Here is where the students wanted to help. Automatically generated sports reports could allow local media to expand coverage and offer more content to their readers, which would enable them to increase the advertising – more articles equal evermore possibilities to place ads. Additionally, it could also free reporters from the chore of writing reviews on all the games in the lower leagues instead of allowing them to focus on more sophisticated analysis and features.

However, much like their predecessors, the weavers, the journalists didn't feel relieved by the automation of parts of their work. Two hundred and seventy-seven years later they too didn't have the impression that the algorithms would disburden them, but were afraid they would replace them. Unlike the weavers they didn't destroy the machines. Instead, the rise of algorithmic help was answered by a wave of indignation. Journalists from Russia to India, from the UK to the US, from Belgium to Italy wrote on the fact that algorithms had learned how to write. Several editorial desks flirted with the end of human journalism altogether. The American magazine *Business Week* worried: 'Are sportswriters really necessary?' *La Stampa* in Italy described journalists 'besieged' by intelligent software. And the Parisian *Le Monde* claimed: 'The era of robot-journalism has begun.' It has.

But what is happening here to journalists will soon happen to everyone: digitalization. Journalism is simply the first profession to experience a change that is much more profound. It will shake up our expertise in general. Far beyond sports reports, algorithms can gather information

DOI: 10.1057/9781137373502

available in data sets or online. Faster than any human, it can restructure the information in a chart, or can even transform its findings into a textual overview. As knowledge has also freed itself from being only available at a specific point, a book in the library or the computer at home, to be available online, a lot of research, reports, and evaluations could be delegated to algorithms. Bankers, lawyers, journalists, all skilled jobs will be affected. Nearly everywhere an employee keeps track of a development; algorithms can draw up an overview instead. It is of no wonder that the university project of a sports report writing algorithm has quickly turned into a start up called 'Narrative Science'. Unsurprisingly it also formed a technology development agreement with the investment firm In-Q-Tel, which supports the CIA and the US Intelligence Community; in the era of digitalization, they surely need help to make sense of today's mountains of collected data.

After disrupting our distribution channels, digitalization reaches out for our production, but this time not just the creative industries will be affected. The disruption caused by finding and creating stories from data will add to the one that shook up traditional ways of distributing music, film, books, or television, but it will quickly reach beyond the creative industries. Business reports, health records, all kinds of summaries can be automated. The technology has the potential to disrupt everything that implies coherent information, and this means: our expertise. Consequently, the social impact of digitalization will be similarly profound to the impact of industrialization, for at present we are a society of experts.

Sociologist Anthony Giddens made the observation some years ago that expertise has become a 'pervasive phenomenon' for now 'an expert is any individual who can successfully lay claim to either specific skills or types of knowledge which the layperson does not possess' (Giddens 1994, 84). More recent studies agree that specialization by field has become the dominant paradigm in education (Amirault and Branson 2006). We are all trained to become experts. Will the effects of digitalization on the middle class be similar to the effects of industrialization on the working class? No matter if you are a lawyer or an accountant, a doctor, a teacher, an engineer, a politician, even a *chef de cuisine*, an author, a car mechanic, a manager, or a micro-chip designer, parts of your skills will soon be taken over by digitalization – and the next chapter will discuss what precisely is happening to experts in great detail. But to start with we should first capture the digital force.

DOI: 10.1057/9781137373502

What are algorithms? How are they defined? And what can they know? The next part will provide a brief overview of academic approaches towards algorithms. Then we will make a short detour back in history to reveal how human knowledge could become a problem in the face of the capabilities of machines. Finally, we will examine what today's algorithms do in order to 'know' – a moment we as experts should better be aware of.

Hidden relationship issues

The text writing algorithms are an indicator that the automation of information has reached its next step. Clearly, the project does mark a turning point, albeit not a beginning – what digitalization might mean for the human race still looms. There will always be more data, different algorithms, new devices, groundbreaking developments, and a next version. In a connected world, things are as challenging as they are complicated. Nonetheless it is high time to start asking questions. As the German philosopher Martin Heidegger once put it, questioning builds a way. This way is needed in order to not simply watch digitalization, but also direct it. So what are algorithms?

In her study of algorithms in architectural and interaction design, the philosopher Luciana Parisi answers this question with a surprising statement. It turns their traditional definition upside down, which goes as follows: algorithms are step-by-step procedures for calculations that consist of instructions and follow a finite set of rules to carry out a computation – a definition dating back to the Persian mathematician Muhammad al'Khwarizmi (pronounced in Latin slang 'algorism'), who had lived c.780–850. But now Parisi writes: 'algorithms are no longer seen as a tool to accomplish a task' (Parisi 2013, XIII). Instead of simply performing rules, she claims that they 'have become performing entities: actualities that select, evaluate, transform, and produce data' (ibid., IX).

Parisi's new approach to algorithms comes at the dawn of a new era. For sure, their computation still consists in sequences of commands that instruct a machine or result (Cormen 2013). For sure, algorithms are still expressed in programming languages such as Java, C++, Python, or Fortran. For sure, they still rely on protocols to exchange communication with other software, devices, or internet nodes. However, in data processing there is an obvious trend to what is generally referred to as

DOI: 10.1057/9781137373502

'big data', that is larger data sets, whose technical history have been well described by Kevin Driscoll (2012). The rise of data, which is technically driven, changes the notion of algorithms profoundly: experts agree that without data to process, the algorithm remains inert (Berry 2011, 33; Cheney-Lippold 2011; Manovich 2013). The effectiveness of algorithms is strongly related to the data sets they compute, and this is even resulting in a dispute: computer scientists (Domingos 2012) as well as businessmen (Croll and Yoskovitz 2013) ponder if more data beat better algorithms, or if it is the other way round.

The humanities take on algorithms has surely been influenced by the data-driven shift. Ever since the British computer scientist Alan Turing (1936) wrote about the idea of a 'Universal Machine', algorithms have fascinated scientists and thinkers alike. His theoretical device, the 'Universal Turing Machine', manipulates symbols, and thereby simulates the logic of a computer algorithm. The young student at King's College Cambridge found that if it is possible to give a mathematical description of the structure of a machine, every machine can be simulated by manipulating symbols. When running a software that consists of algorithms, his 'universal' principle comes to life. And as this life is generally described as 'virtual', the status of the algorithm is a complicated and highly interesting issue for philosophers.

The term 'algorithm' belongs to one language family with 'code', the language of our time, and one could say: code is the language in which an algorithm is written. Both describe the same 'thing' from a different perspective: the word 'algorithm' – a set of rules to be followed by calculations – marks a mathematical perspective, while the word 'code' – a system of words to represent others – takes a linguistic perspective. Similarly to its name, its ontological status – what is its being? – has been approached from various sides:

▸ As inexistent: The German media theorist Friedrich Kittler famously claims 'There is no software' (1995). In his description, algorithms are a sheer effect of the hardware they rely on, designed to disguise our technical hardware determination. While this is a radical approach of some beauty, it also offers various problems: from a philosophical perspective, it repeats the gesture of idealistic philosophy to seek truth behind a curtain; from a humanistic perspective, it operates along the lines of technological determinism; from a pragmatic perspective, it lacks an approach to study the evolving field of software further. Against Kittler,

DOI: 10.1057/9781137373502

Andrew Goffey (2008) has demonstrated the many ways in which an algorithm executes 'control'.

▸ As an activity: Kittler scholar Wolfgang Ernst focuses on the fact that an algorithm stores information in a different way than writing: breaking it down in 0 and 1, it doesn't narrate but counts. Therefore, archives in the age of online digital collections become a 'mathematically defined space' (cf. Ernst 2012; Parikka 2011). Shintaro Miyazaki (2012) also emphasizes the activity, but insists that in a strict sense it is not even mathematical. In his view, an algorithm formulated in a programming language is not the same as an algebraic formula: it is not 'recursive'. Alexander Galloway stresses the specific ontological quality of algorithms and code as executable: 'code is the summation of language plus an executable metalayer that encapsulates that language' (Galloway 2004, 165). While the ontological status of an algorithm as process has been acknowledged, the approach has also been questioned. Against the tendency to treat source code as an origin from which algorithmic actions emerge, Chun (2008 and 2013) makes the point that interfaces are more than the effect of their source.

▸ As an interaction: Software studies look further into the algorithmic activity in a broader sense and seek to overcome the 'immateriality' of software (Fuller 2008, 4). Aspects of design, glitches, interactions, or preferences come into focus (Fuller 2003), as well as the social condition of the algorithm's production (Berry 2011, 43–51). Software can only be understood in the middle of things: 'we can only begin with things' (Chun 2008, 324). While her approach widens the view, it is criticized from the perspective of the Kittler school as falling back into a technological oblivion.

▸ As things: Like Chun (2013, 8), philosopher Yuk Hui takes the relation between algorithms and things a step further. Addressing data as a 'digital object' and relating it to the philosophical discourse of things, he notes that 'the evolution of technical standards from GML to XML to Web ontologies blurs the distinction between a simple text file and a structured computer program' (Hui 2012, 394). Next to 'natural objects' discussed in continental philosophy, next to the 'technical object' discussed in Simondon's philosophy of technology, the new ontological status of a 'digital object' emerges. The digital object is defined by relations: 'relationality is the point where algorithms act' (394). Parisi likewise

DOI: 10.1057/9781137373502

talks of 'algorithmic objects', to push philosophical thinking further: inspired by the computer scientist's Chaitin's findings of a constant that is definable but not computable, she locates them 'transverse to both, the mathematical and the physical domain' (Parisi 2013, 5).

▸ As useful instruments: In the humanities, algorithms are not only reflected upon but also used. To analyse culture in a new way, large data sets are compiled and digitalized material is visualized. The cultural analytic Lev Manovich (2013) develops visualization tools to analyse videos on the level of specific frames. The literary scholar Franco Moretti (2005) uses quantitative methods to generate a graph of the fast rise and dramatic fall of British novelistic genres (44 genres over 160 years), or maps the radically changing geography in village narratives. The new ways of generating cultural knowledge, by combining quantitative methods with data sets and algorithms, are referred to as 'Digital Humanities' (cf. Berry 2012; Lunenfeld et al. 2012). Here, algorithms give rise not just to the perspective 'understanding culture through digital technology' as David Berry (2012, 5) puts it. Exploring algorithms, he points out, is essential for today's 'knowing knowledge' (6). While the approach makes creative use of algorithms and can be seen as an important step to know more about today's knowledge, it is also criticized to reduce algorithms to a sheer instrumental role, answered by Alan Liu (2012) with a sympathetic and important call to rethink the idea of instrumentality.

When looking at how algorithms warp the field of knowledge in unprecedented ways, these definitions should be kept in mind. They surely influence the question this chapter now goes further into: How do algorithms reshape knowledge?

Fuelling the historical event of digitalization, today computers go beyond computing. In order to learn how to 'write' they start to 'know', a characterization that causes us immediately to furrow our brows. Isn't it that computers process 'information', while 'knowledge' is information that has been further processed and understood by humans? For sure, one is tempted to maintain one's ground that the order of things hasn't changed. But we also sense that something has happened. How can we grasp this shift? The Oxford Dictionaries define 'information' as 'facts provided...about something or someone' compared to 'knowledge', which is 'facts, information or skills acquired through experience or education'. Thus, we can say knowledge is processed information. In this

DOI: 10.1057/9781137373502

case, however, it seems like algorithms are by now educated or experienced enough to enter the next stage: they are operating on a level at which information isn't simply reproduced. Instead they sort, classify, and compile information; that is they process it to add meaning. Hereby they turn information into the skill we usually describe as, well, knowledge. Did we now truly create a ghost in the machine?

By reporting pure facts they can produce any story that is following a template. Similarly to the devices and machines of the industrial revolution, they are simplifying working procedures, replacing workforce, but also opening up new areas. Generating college game reports no salaried journalist had written about before was the start for sports reporting algorithms such as Stats Monkey, or its alternative StatSheet. Here, both projects clearly reach out to areas where coverage is of some interest, though not profit-yielding for a human writer. Nonetheless as the international headlines show, they eventually invoked a debate, and the template of the debate seems to be borrowed straight from industrialization: man vs machine.

A look at our competitive relationship with machines is quite interesting. The debate can't be settled. The race is a tie. A computer is faster, a human is more creative, and both, machine and man, are prone to mistakes: while facts and numbers don't tell the whole story, human observation can distort things, too. Numbers and statistics play an important role in a sports report, hence it is a perfect set for digital innovation as stories still function when they are pared down to the bare bones. Sports – often belittled as the toy department – always was a sphere open to the tool or the machine, sometimes to the extent that it becomes fuzzy, what can be ascribed to the man and what to the equipment. Soon this will be said of reporting, too, and while some of us ponder if a human can put more colours into a text than an algorithm, other humans reprogram the algorithm to reach out for a fan quote posted on the internet: fuzzy borders (Grier 2005). More importantly, though: Is this really a rat race between the man and machine? Invoking a survival of the fittest might simply be choosing the wrong template, and beside the point. A threat is tangible; it has been clearly articulated by the journalists. But is it the machine that is threatening the human? Technology is not neutral and surely imposes its own logic upon us, but that doesn't mean we can abdicate our responsibility. For all we know, the machine isn't interested in dominating; it isn't a human. Digitalization is happening, but its logic can be interpreted in many different ways. To understand this paradox is

DOI: 10.1057/9781137373502

the aim of this book. Where does our hostile reaction towards technology come from?

Let's dig into history by visiting the Royal Society in London on February 1, 1673. Ever since machines learned to calculate in the seventeenth century, they were treated as if they were capable of sapience of the *homo sapiens*, but much like the mind, which let's us down from time to time, the machine presented to some members at the Royal Society on the first of February wasn't working properly yet. The idea, though, was already alive. The mechanical age discussed the mind as functioning like an automaton. The versatile scholar Gottfried Wilhelm Leibniz, who had brought his machine with him to London's Royal Society, thought in particular that language could be seen as a mirror of the mind.

> If words were constructed according to a device that I see possible, but which those who have built universal languages have not discovered, we could arrive at the desired result by means of words themselves, a feat which would be of incredible utility for human life. (Leibniz 1951, 51–52)

Leibniz considered the formulation of an artificial language composed of symbols that imitate the axioms we supposedly make use of in reasoning. While for him our brain was occupied with all sorts of things, our mind was only busy with operations of understanding and intelligence. The mind was the pure instrument of thinking, exploring, and reasoning. Thus reason wasn't simply given but an exceptional condition of the brain, and could be proved. Inspired by the calculator of inventor Blaise Pascal, Leibniz constructed the wooden model of a digital mechanical machine. This subset of an artificial intelligence, the 'Stepped Reckoner', was presented at the Royal Society in London on February 1, 1673. Although it didn't work yet, Leibniz received some encouragement for it, and Sir Robert Moray put him forward for a fellowship of the Society. It was the machine for the dawn of a new discourse: the age of reason. The philosopher Gilbert Ryle (1949, 8–9) describes its approach later as follows: the workings of our minds must follow equal laws as the mechanical laws; and mechanical laws explain movements in space as the effects of other movements in space. For Leibniz and his contemporaries, machines such as stepped reckoners made it possible to explore the workings of the minds, that is the laws of reason in particular and human intelligence in general. The exploration should keep philosophers busy for quite a while, among others a very angry Ryle, who refuted the addressing of body and mind as separate entities and called it a

DOI: 10.1057/9781137373502

'category-mistake' responsible for the creation of a 'Ghost in the Machine' (Ryle 1949, 22).

Indeed, the ghost had turned out to be even a monster: the idea of the mind functioning like an automaton had become a big problem when the machines had speeded up and left the mind behind. When computers finally took over from the mechanical machines, the idea that there is artificial intelligence had already evolved. Consequently the relation between computer hardware and computer software was set analogous to the division of body and mind. It seems that a more complicated scholarly debate filling bookshelves in libraries as well as centuries wasn't available. Admittedly the idea of an intelligent machine has some gravitational force: developing an intelligent agent that can replace the human is still a military hope in which the US army invested millions. In the arts and in entertainment, the idea of an intelligent machine also leaves some impressions. The end of the *Homo sapiens* has been averted on the screen in productions as various as *2001 Space Odyssey*, *Terminator*, *Matrix*, or the series *Battlestar Galactica*. In the game 'Jeopardy!', however, machines have finally overcome mankind: in 2011 IBM's supercomputer Watson defeats his human competitors to win $1 million. Are machines the better, non-fallible humans? Can they actually think like we do? Or even better? Let's turn to the doings of the machines.

In the beginning of the computer age, the machines' cognitive ability was promising until the progress of the rather expensive supercomputers stopped. By the 1970s, the failures of machine translation and speech comprehension research had clearly started to annoy the American technology agency Defense Advanced Research Projects Agency (DARPA), and the frustration was echoed by the Lighthill report for the British Science Research Council from 1973. Enthusiasm and with it financing ceased. Philosophers, among others Ryle, first challenged the idea of the mind as a functioning automaton, and then attacked the idea of artificial intelligence. By the time the American philosopher Hubert L. Dreyfus successfully stirred up a fierce discussion on artificial intelligence about 'What Computer's can't do' (Dreyfus 1972) – think, for example – the so called winter of artificial intelligence had set in. Later, one of Dreyfus's colleagues, the philosopher John Searle, would introduce a thought experiment that was due to explain why computing is different from thinking while having the same effects. The experiment is known as the Chinese Room.

DOI: 10.1057/9781137373502

In brief, it describes a monolingual English speaker who is locked in a room and given a large batch of Chinese writing, plus a set of rules on how to operate Chinese signs in English. While the speaker doesn't understand a word of Chinese, his answers are indistinguishable from those of Chinese speakers. This, explains Searle, is what a computer does. A computer follows rules, but it doesn't understand. Superiority of the human: saved. Of course, Searle's and Dreyfus's critique of artificial reason annoyed computer scientists, but they freed the human from being out-distanced by a machine; it is an irony of fate that most computers today are assembled in China according to rules of largely monolingual English speakers. What must be understood and can be learned from following Leibniz's idea of artificial intelligence from the Royal Society all the way up to the computer discourse of the last century, however, is that it wasn't the machine that unnerved the human with being outdistanced.

Not the machines, but our ideas about it were in our way – and as the machines are about to strike again, we can assume that the problem will return. In fact, the idea that humans have been surpassed by computers is absurd. Machines never set fallible humans against non-fallible computers. Anyone who ever spilled coke over a keyboard and a humanoid arm knows which of them is more resilient. Supercomputers are even more fragile. In the beginning, they were to be locked away from their own programmers into sterile air-conditioned environments (Breheim 1961). Consequently, we should prick up our ears when the sports report writing algorithm instantly evokes the old pattern of man vs. machine. We should become suspicious. While back then the machine was seen as the better, more reasonable human, today the human is seen as the bet-ter, more creative machine. By comparing man with machine, we reduce the human to the logic of being effective, and this inhuman logic needs to be interrupted. It can be, by refusing a comparison that describes the human in a purely capitalistic logic. The question whether a human is more creative than a machine is a fatal approach. Humans aren't creative machines, and machines are not interested in competing with man on who is more effective.

Nevertheless it is true: algorithms are changing our world. As they become an integral part of our world, algorithms re-organize knowledge. This changes what it is 'to think' as much as the machine redirected in the nineteenth century what it was 'to work', and both give no reason to throw one's hands up in technophobic despair. Without doubt being terrified has been of use in evolution, but it is not always the best response. Besides, the

DOI: 10.1057/9781137373502

change of 'brain work' is nothing new in history. Thinking and memory itself is, so to say, historical. It is a technique which Plato described as the action of 'division and collection', when he made Socrates address dialectics as a tool that helps him 'to speak and to think' (Plato 2005, 266b). In history, this technique has been trained differently. In the earlier days of education, for example, the emphasis was on training your mind through memorization. Then enlightenment introduced the idea that students should not only know but also understand the facts. Now, the student had to 'have courage to use your own understanding' 'without the guidance of another', as the German philosopher Kant (1787, 1) put it in his answer to the question 'What is enlightenment?' As a matter of fact, the German King Frederick the Great brought this advice quite literally into play. In 1770 he gave explicit order to the professors of the German universities to command their students to 'think for themselves' (Bosse 1990, 61–62). Then thinking changed again: books such as the *Encyclopaedia Britannica* first published between 1768 and 1771 in Edinburgh were about to become a device to store facts in order to assist our uninformed memories. Now digitalization is shifting the storage, but compared to the lexical entry the new digital form 'search result' gets regarded as 'shallow' – a concern that media critic Nicholas Carr put in a nutshell in his essay: 'Is Google Making Us Stupid?' (Carr 2008).

The essay as well as his book *The Shallows: How the Internet Is Changing the Way We Think, Read and Remember* (Carr 2010) argue that due to information overload and constant distraction by our digital devices, we lose the ability to concentrate and find ourselves threatened with regress to a primitive state of distraction. Carr finds this reinforced by developments in neuroscience, which addresses the brain not anymore as a fixed structure. Brain plasticity has been studied since the late 1970s, and became widely known when in 2000 the American neuropsychiatrist Eric Kandel was awarded with others a Nobel prize for studies showing that memory storage relies on modifications in synaptic connections. The idea of brain plasticity, philosophically explored by Catherine Malabou (2008), not only allowed freedom from genetic determinism, but also made our brain dependent from its use. As Carr puts it: 'We become, neurologically, what we think' (2010, 33). Replacing our memory with the use of search engines, he concluded that mankind is threatened with 'intellectual decay' (21 and 35). Carr's concern found an overwhelming echo. Within weeks, the question got picked up by media all over the world, among them *The Observer*, the German weekly magazine *Der*

DOI: 10.1057/9781137373502

Spiegel; it was written about in *The Wall Street Journal*, discussed by the *BBC*, found on Dutch blogs, and in French magazines. From there, it took its place at dinner table conversations, entered lunch breaks, to be adjourned, finally, to the pub. But is thinking with algorithms really deteriorating our knowledge?

History teaches us that our societies have always welcomed new media with suspicion. This is why we have to ask ourselves if the evidence summarized by Nicholas Carr can also be read in another way. Fortunately, Carr's essay has provoked many interesting answers not only in public media but also in academia. Among those we find Katherine Hayles's intelligent arguments about *How We Think* (2012), a book in which she analyses the material cited by Carr anew. She comes to a very different conclusion: instead of degenerating, we simply adapt to what and how we need to know in an information rich environment. Hayles writes:

> In contemporary digital environments, the information explosion of the web has again made an exponentially greater number of texts available dwarfing the previous amount of print materials by several orders of magnitude. (2012, 62)

In addition to that, Rob Lucas's elaborate 'New Left Review' essay on Carr clarifies the role of a technology that might have 'augmented our mental capabilities and transformed them' (Lucas 2012, 65), but also leaves some manoeuvring room: 'the problems of this mind are not merely technical, but also social and economic. They are also political' (ibid., 68). Technology isn't imposing its logic on our brains; its logic can be shaped. Finally, Michael Wheeler (2011) picks up the point following Andy Clark's (and Donna Haraway's) assumption of human beings as 'natural cyborgs', coming to a very different conclusion than Carr. Discussing the use of a calculator in an academic test, he points out the following: what might qualify as cheating in one situation might be perfectly acceptable in another. The intellectual decay is, so to say, to a certain extent in the eye of its beholder. What it is 'to think', changes over time – recently, the philosopher Bernard Stiegler (2010) has shown how cognitive capitalism is taking advantage of our current version of thinking. Turning to anthropology, we find evidence that the technique and technology by which we manipulate signs has always influenced not only how we think but also what kind of thinking we value. The French anthropologist André Leroi-Gourhan, once a colleague of the young philosopher Jacques Derrida, even considers writing as the third memory

DOI: 10.1057/9781137373502

of man, besides the DNA and the brain (Leroi-Gourhan 1993, 257ff). By using and manipulating signs, humans can enhance their skills and their creativity. Following this approach, we can notice that his third memory is about to restructure itself as digitalization shifts the field of writing and thinking. From this point of view, digitalizing knowledge isn't making us stupid. Search can be understood as a new mode of knowing that makes use of different mental abilities. Instead of feeling threatened by machines, we can comprehend the new way of reason. Instead of simply letting digitalization happen, while being content to quarrel with one's loss, we can shape it to our advantage and the advantage of our societies – events can't be undone, but they can be directed. For this we need to understand how digitalization transforms the order of knowledge. Let's have a look at how algorithms operate language.

Looking into the clouds

The scientists of the Intelligence Information Laboratory from the Northwestern University didn't just program algorithms for sports report, they also made them to review movies. For this the algorithms had to learn how to crib as they need to mine existing utterances on the internet which are put into a spoken dialogue between two animated slackers called Zack and Zooey. To serve these virtual anchors, the script first looks up the name of a movie online at the Internet Movie Database, where it learns details about the director, the actors, and so on. Then the algorithms make use of movie review aggregation sites such as Rotten Tomatoes or Metacritic, platforms that collect different reviews of one and the same movie to give cinephiles an unbiased overview. Here, the script simply counts the scores of different reviewers, to figure out its judgment about a movie, and displays the outcome in one of three dialogue templates: generally positive or negative reviews, and a divergent one in case the critics disagree. It fills out these templates by taking introductory snippets of reviews, which will be further sorted into a set of statements: positive and negative statements about the director, leading actor, supporting actor, and so on. From this set finally a dialogue gets calculated: algo critic one says something positive about the movie and the leading actor, algo critic two disagrees and says something negative about the leading actor. Or algo critic one says something negative about the leading actor and algo critic two endorses that with another

DOI: 10.1057/9781137373502

negative comment whereby the algorithms pick fragments with words that haven't been found in the first set in order for the critics not to repeat each other.

In the early test runs it becomes quickly apparent that the algorithms have no clue what they are talking about – as if to prove Searle's Chinese Room experiment. Instead of smoothly digesting the online found bits, they rather seem to choke on nuggets of information that are way too big:

> Tom Cruise stars with Carice van Houten and Kenneth Branagh in the film Valkyrie. In this PG-13 rated drama, based on actual events, a plot to assassinate Hitler is unfurled during the height of WWII.

To then suddenly break with the austere style and burst out in the middle of the war:

> I have to tell you, I loved this movie. The movie works like a clock. (Nichols, Gandy, and Hammond 2009)

As long as stuttering algorithms explode information about mediocre movies enthusiastically in our face, the reputation of a 'machine brain' for being able to process language will stay damaged, and the so-called winter of artificial intelligence will continue. Still, the technology should be taken serious. What can be digitalized? Like the 1966 created computer therapist ELIZA, Apple's personal assistant application Siri, which was launched on their mobile phones on October 4, 2011, is talking to us quite fluently. But when processing continuous text, algorithms meet their technical limits. Machines will never 'understand'. Nonetheless a thaw has set in, which could in the future take the experiment further. Digitalization is transforming different aspects of knowledge: from the growing range of digitalized information, to the ability of automatically linking or comparing different knowledge fields, to new forms of accessing knowledge. There is new hope that machines might not need to understand meaning anymore in order to automate information. These aspects deserve to be looked into in more detail.

The statistical learning of machines, for example, has increased, so that not only machine translation but also speech recognition – both former problem children of artificial intelligence – have made impressive progress. As knowledge is converted digitally, algorithms can calculate the disparate language field related to a world, in order to scale its meaning more precise. This is needed because words like to disobey. They change their meaning in different contexts. 'I have sinned', for

DOI: 10.1057/9781137373502

example, could be a religious request to ask for forgiveness after having done something wrong; it could refer to a pun ascribed to the British General Charles John Napier, when he announced the conquest of the Province of Sindh in 1840; it could be the title of the political speech given by President Bill Clinton on the September 11, 1998 answering the Starr Report dealing with his concealing of a relationship with former White House intern Monica Lewinsky.

As huge amounts of language have been digitalized with the internet, the computer can now capture different relations of a word by calculating its possible meaning with a statistical comparison of diverse textual contexts. This is the reason for companies such as Google not only to analyse websites or emails, but also scan and photocopy millions of books. As more data is a presupposition for a better statistical understanding, they accumulate digital data as if they were a party of squirrels preparing to spend the winter. And in order to survive this winter and see the artificial digital spring again, Google is sorting the mass of written and spoken language. However, the abundance of knowledge online is immediately causing new problems: the field of knowledge accessible for algorithms is vaster than ever before. In a certain way one could say that as much as the weaving device of the 'Flying Shuttle' speeded up the process of weaving thereby creating the demand for the 'Spinning Jenny', the vast knowledge now digitalized produces the demand for new algorithms: a new request for overviews and for sorting information.

For this force of digitalization search engines themselves are good examples: Yahoo!, for example, started as a collection of favourite webpages, and after it was launched professionally, its web directories were still maintained by humans. As the masses entered the web, however, to leave innumerable homepages behind, even an army of humans had no chance of indexing the internet anymore. It became too successful. The amount of webpages exploded. There needed to be a new way of indexing the internet. A website's relevance had to be registered automatically. Sergei Brin and Lawrence Page introduced this to the digital public with Google, when presenting their paper 'The Anatomy of a Large-Scale Hypertextual Web Search Engine' at a conference in 1998 (Brin and Page 1998). Their approach was new and different. Here, the algorithms are breaking down a complicated metric considering more than hundreds of millions of variables by using probability distribution. In principle, part of these equations analyse the content – URL, name of a page, words in the headline, captions, continuous text and so on, as well as the

DOI: 10.1057/9781137373502

publishing date; others take the success of a page into account assisted by a trick: the 'PageRank', an algorithm that is named after its creator. Its equation doesn't just count how often a page is linked to. It also evaluates the source of the link in order to weigh information institutions such as *The Economist* or *The Guardian* with a higher relevance, and picks out fake links simply set up to make a page look successful – the algorithms try to calculate human orientation for a trustworthy source.

While the algorithms are trained to imitate human understanding, the human usage of the internet shifts. In the beginning, search engines are used to look for information on the internet. But soon they are regarded as an index of the world, and turned towards to whenever one is in need of knowledge. Besides the online-lexicon Wikipedia launched in 2001, innumerable 'How-To-pages', by then a paying concern, revealed our desire to get some online advice for just about everything from building an igloo to knotting a tie. However, knowledge on the internet often has a different status: compared to its predecessor the encyclopaedia, knowledge on the internet isn't presented as a canonical fact. Digitalization changes the status of knowledge: While Wikipedia can always be changed, a search machine organizes the knowledge neatly beaded in a list. The query doesn't deliver an institutionalized answer or finds the institutionalized webpage, but delivers a number of competing voices. To evaluate these voices, we users are often asked for our opinion. In fact ranking or driving user engagement by implementing a like or dislike button is an omnipresent feature on the internet. With the technical functionality of ranking, a piece of information gets evaluated whereby an additional parameter is put on, hence providing the algorithms with orientation. Here, the logic of digitalization driven by human usage introduces an interesting shift: knowledge is now voted upon. What has been described as a 'democratization of information' changes what gets to be known: on the internet, information isn't correct or false; it gets balloted, and is thereby made found or doomed to vanish. Or is the internet simply making apparent what has been common practice for quite a while now?

In our industrial past, something became a fact, an achievement, or evidence, when scientific institutions incorporated it in their canon, until newer facts, achievements, or evidences officially replaced this truth (Arendt 1958, 290). That isn't the case anymore. It is not the authoritarian voice of an institution that crowns the status quo of a scientific finding. Ever since the peer review became central, academic

DOI: 10.1057/9781137373502

knowledge has been evaluated by several qualified individuals. This choir of experts is voting on what shall become academic knowledge. Here, a fact is not given but made, when the majority of the experts confirm it. In an ideal world the confirmation isn't established by addressing the bland mainstream, instead it's the plurality that is decisive: something is regarded as 'true' when it stays consistent in the plurality of expert opinions and has been confirmed in different perspectives. On a philosophical level we can say that what is considered as 'truth' unveils itself in a new form. As truths are everlasting and therefore more permanent than all matter of facts ever will be, we can never be certain. Truths can always only be approached. Nonetheless truths obviously have happily lifted their old-fashioned veils and left their untouchable thrones in order to hide in a new home: plurality. Thus, we can say that this new order of knowledge exceeds digitalization, but becomes apparent with it. It is older than digitalization, but put into play by it. And as our digital present plays according to its rules, let's have a look at the game and its various aspects.

First, we have seen that in search, digital information isn't delivered as an institutional fact, but needs to be assessed by the users. Search engines help with the evaluation, when the choir of voices on the internet gets neatly bundled into a list. Despite its ranking, however, the list seems to be nothing but a provisional proposal we need to make sense of ourselves. When we access the material and find consistency with several independent links presenting the same outcome, only then we transform search results to knowledge. Here it becomes apparent that plurality is an essential factor in today's truth finding. In the digital era, it can be found in many ways.

One fact, for example, leads to a plurality of other aspects. The computational knowledge engine WolframAlpha, an online service that uses vast data sets of reliable information from trusted scientific sources to extract 'new' knowledge, makes use of facts in this different way. It generates knowledge by combining or comparing a query with a fact's contextual knowledge thereby taking the cross-reference that was used in the lexical denoting to a new level. When asked 'Where is the moon?' WolframAlpha automatically relates 'moon' to my current location telling me that it is currently not visible in 'London, Greater London', but places it with altitude and Azimuth in the current sky position also providing its astronomical constellation 'Libra' as well as moonrise and moonset. Here plurality turns in a different role, that of the plurality

DOI: 10.1057/9781137373502

of facts, as WolframAlpha falls back upon its richness of data. It hosts information ranging from geographical data to sports history, from weather information to the position of a planet, from the global warming potential of methane to national statistics, from biological facts to business performances.

Wolfram Alpha, however, isn't just openly hosting those sets; it takes the information one step further. All of its data sets have been translated into the symbolic mathematical language *Mathematica* thereby combining the once isolated facts. Asked 'What was the weather like when Tony Blair was born?', it matches historic weather data with Blair's date of birth: on May 6, 1953 it had an average of 14° and a low cloud cover during the day until 6 pm with a humidity of 71%. Combining or comparing contextual facts can also produce data narratives. Asked after 'nuclear warheads', WolframAlpha indicates that for the year 2012 there are about 23,4000 of them on earth to then add more information to it: Russia is leading the stockpile rankings with 13,000 followed by the US with 9,400, while France is placed a distant third with 300 followed by others. Is the cold war secretly continuing? Do all the current news about nuclear ambitions of other countries simply give themselves an air of importance thereby hiding the actual power constellation? – Another example: Asked if the there are more sheep in the UK or in the US, the result is that in the year 2009 there were 30.8m sheep in the UK and only 5.75m in the US. The visualization, however, also reveals that the UK livestock of sheep declined dramatically at the end of 1970s. Eight million sheep were vanishing, answered by a steep rise of its livestock ten years later to 45 million. Did Prime Minister Margaret Thatcher have not only a down on British miners? Or did a killer disease infect the lovely ball of wool?

Finally, accessing the facts is also changing. With the mobile internet rose a ubiquitous access to knowledge. In effect, knowledge has left its traditional central medium of storage and transportation, the book, to enter an omnipresent digital layer that coats our world. After digitalization spread from the computer to the phone into the digital cloud, the cloud is following you wherever you are, a joy that sometimes feels like the curse of King Midas: everything we touch, film or record, is stored as data and uploaded on the internet. After centuries of good cooperation, knowledge has broken faith with its traditional medium, the book. Instead your position becomes the new page on which

DOI: 10.1057/9781137373502

digitalization displays its information: The Washington DC based Sunlight Foundation, for example, built an application which displayed where the $787 billion were going, which the US government spent in the American Recovery and Reinvestment act of 2009 to resuscitate the economy. Using the augmented reality platform Layar, the app visualized the financial information, breaking it down on the location around the user, to explore the closest recipients of the money. When testing the application, an expert from the technology magazine *ReadWriteWeb* noticed with amazement some political bias – for example, that in Portland an auto shop and a Bible college had received more money then an eco-car company, a Native American youth program, or even a technical college.

Paradoxically apps such as these enable a plurality of crucial details to come out into the light. At the same time they virtualize knowledge. The new order of omnipresent access to knowledge is based on a fundamental difference to our paper past when, apart from travel guides, reading was done in special surroundings in order to be able to learn and be roughly memorized. Now knowledge does not have to be known, but it is to be activated. For this, our current location or view is used as a medium on which to apply the information by means of GPS navigation, a visual picture search, or augmented reality applications. At the beginning of the twentieth century the German philosopher Walter Benjamin had noticed something similar, when he described how writing was changing its status.

> Writing, having found shelter in the printed book, where it was leading an independent existence, is ruthlessly dragged out into the street by advertisements and subjected to the brutal heteronomies of economic chaos. Such are the harsh schooldays of its new form. Centuries ago it began gradually to record itself, passing from erect inscription to the slanting script of hands resting on desks and eventually bedding down in book-printing; now, with equal slowness, it is beginning once again to rise from the floor. Even today's newspapers are already scanned more from top to bottom than horizontally; films and posters are completing the process, pushing script into the dictatorial vertical. Before contemporary man gets to open a book, so dense a flurry of changeable, brightly coloured, clashing characters has settled on his eyes that the chances of his penetrating the ancient silence of the book have become slim. Locust swarms of lettering, already darkening the sun of the supposed mind of the city dweller, become thicker with each successive year. (Benjamin 2009, 66)

DOI: 10.1057/9781137373502

With digitalization, this development intensified. The time, when writing found asylum in the book, has come to an end. Soon knowledge will get delivered in applications as much as in books and documents. From 'monkey with skull' to 'monkey with phone': Today, the sculpture of Hugo Rheinhold that once stood on Vladimir Lenin's desk, an ape sitting on a pile of books of which the spine of one reads 'Darwin', would not cradle its chin with the contemplative gesture of his left hand, while looking at the skull; it would use it to hold a mobile phone surfing for information about it. However, the ape would still need to make use of its own reasoning, even though it shifts from 'knowing it' to 'knowing about'. As our findings above have shown, the shift could be summed up as follows:

▶ Instead of one authority that affirms something as a fact, there is now a choir of voices, in whose plurality information needs to stay consistent to be considered as factual.
▶ Digital facts are bound to be related to other facts and can be displayed in varying visualizations.
▶ Even though digital information now coats our world wherever we are, we need to know about it, in order to be able to activate it.

In the first chapter, we analysed the digitalization first of language, then of knowledge to illustrate that a new theme – plurality – has entered our discourse. By this, the principle that organizes knowledge, truth, has captured a new notion; one could say that truth gets haunted by its plural. However, for the notion of knowledge, change is nothing new. The enlightenment shifted the evaluation of truth and information from the beliefs of the middle age to reason, and from religion to science, thus from contemplation to action. As Hannah Arendt registers: 'truth was no longer supposed to appear, to reveal and disclose itself to the mental eye of a beholder', instead there 'arose a veritable necessity to hunt for truth behind deceptive appearances' (Arendt 1958, 290). With digitalization, the art of hunting down truth changes again. Back then, knowledge ceased to be seen as a revealed insight, but became a fabricated fact focused upon being, once set right, eternally reproducible. A product. Now the product is dealt with in plural, to become contingent showing relevant possibilities. Here, the shape of truth seems to be related to the technical means we use for approaching it. Certainly, processing facts digitally does alter our approach to knowledge – a search engine doesn't know more than an individual, but on average it surely has wider

DOI: 10.1057/9781137373502

access to information. With this, it transforms the fundament of democratic Western societies – it is not only money that fuels our economy. Information and knowledge are a means of production and play an equal role. In meetings, projects, briefings, reports, appointments, conferences, and press releases employees and experts are managing information. Even jobs that aren't done in offices often involve computers. Workers need to know how to operate the machines of production, instead of using their physical strength. Now algorithms organize knowledge and write. This chapter has focused on the transformation of knowledge. The next chapter takes a detailed look at the effect of this transformation on our society of experts. Will digitalization be to our large middle class what industrialization was to the proletariat?

Are experts outdated now that a digitalization has flooded the field of knowledge with information? Or will old facts soon be treated as precious antiques? And who dictates that we always have to be up to date?

DOI: 10.1057/9781137373502

2
How the Automation of Knowledge Changes Skilled Work

Abstract: *This chapter contributes to sociology of labour by analysing knowledge work and the role of an expert in the digital era. For this, it critically discusses two assumptions: (1) The confusion of technology with capitalism: Looking at statistic developments as well as into political discussions of labour by Negri, Žižek, or Berardi, it finds that technology gets often blamed for capitalistic exploitation. However, as the chapter shows capitalistic logic is not identical with the machines. (2) The definition of technology as secondary knowledge: Philosophical concepts of technology often understood it as practical knowledge, which puts it in a derivative and inferior position. Against understanding technical knowledge in opposition to cultural knowledge, the French philosopher Gilbert Simondon defines it in continuation. Taking up his perspective, the relation of technology and knowledge can be approached anew as 'knowing with': the expert thinks together with the machines; the machines exceed the capitalistic logic.*

Keywords: Sociology of labour, digital labour, skilled labour, expert, capitalism, exploitation, 'philosophy of technology', 'technology and knowledge', 'knowing with', Gilbert Simondon

Mercedes Bunz. *The Silent Revolution: How Digitalization Transforms Knowledge, Work, Journalism and Politics Without Making Too Much Noise.* Basingstoke: Palgrave Macmillan, 2014. DOI: 10.1057/9781137373502.

In our post-industrial societies, information and knowledge became the decisive factor of working life. Regardless whether we are teachers or CEOs, parents or interactive designers, chefs or car mechanics, journalists or politicians, scientists or shop assistants, judges or criminals, our self-conception is that of being an expert. Now digitalization steals our knowledge. What will be left for us to do? Industrialization and technical progress have already emptied the industrial facilities of humans. Now technology suffers all the noise, the heat, and the unhealthy conditions as the poetic documentaries of the filmmaker Harun Farocki (2009) show: manpower, that is physical strength, sequences of movements, handcraft, or the finishing touch still play a part, but they don't rule the scene anymore. Alongside the assembly lines, objects dance around on their own, having a human visitor only from time to time to check that everything is behaving well and all is in order.

The machines produce for us, and we humans have migrated somewhere else. We work in knowledge and service sectors such as transport and tourism, technology and bio-science, banking and financial services, wholesaling and retailing, education and health care, legal services, information products, and entertainment. Here, we produce intangible goods with our immaterial labour. Our work is project-oriented and not focused towards any end product. Our production is not based on physical strength but on knowledge. Now the machines process faster and know better. Does this mean, history is repeating? Are text writing algorithms indicating an automatization of knowledge in a similar way to the machines that automatized the workforce a decade ago? Will there be a sequel to the film 'Workers Leaving the Factory'? Will the algorithms drive us experts out of the service industry? Where can we go from here?

At the beginning of this century, the industrial sector provided only about 25% of the total Western workforce while immaterial production increased to an average of 70%. With the rise of the robots in the 1970s, industrial production as the former carthorse of modern economies was overtaken by knowledge transformed into a new product named 'service'; back then Daniel Bell and other sociologists coined the term 'post-industrial society' (Bell 1974). And post-industrial they remained: detailed figures of the world bank for 2008 show 76.9% of UK's employers working within this tertiary sector of immaterial work, a figure that rises even to 86% in the US, while Sweden employs 76%, France 72.9%, Spain 67.9%, and Russia 61.8%. Everywhere in Western societies, even

DOI: 10.1057/9781137373502

in France very proud of their 400 distinct types of cheese, agriculture comes in last with about 2–4%.

The former tertiary sector of the economy became clearly the leader. We are dependent on our knowledge: expertise and not physical strength is the contribution the well-educated middle class brings to the workplace. To become an expert, we have acquired knowledge from education, through an apprenticeship, or by being an intern learning a lesson in the important game of office hierarchies while we have been sent to handle the printer or photocopying machine, today's equivalents of 'filing' or 'emptying the paper basket'. But not only the work of the intern, also knowledge has changed: offices still come with a swivel chair, but administration has turned from bureaucracy into complex communication. Expert thinking focuses on non-routine tasks. Now next to the chair the knowledge swivels. Still, one gets the impression that the sociologist Max Weber, known for his criticism of society's bureaucratization (Weber 1905), would not be pleased by the fact that creativity instead of rationalization became an asset of the office, and not only because the algorithms have learned how to write. All work, even the play? Some think so and speak of a 'rise of the creative class' (Boltanski and Chiapello 2005; Florida 2002), others describe this development as 'the soul at work' (Berardi 2009), and state that we live in the age of immaterial labour or knowledge work (Hardt and Negri 2004, 184–186; Lazzarato 1997). Which seems to be the case: while middle-income range shifts from place to place, the fact that the members of the middle class are well educated is an absolute term. Regarding work, expertise has become the key aspect in our middle-class societies. And now digitalization is stealing the key.

When the economists Brynjolfsson and McAfee examined the recovery from the recession for their short, yet important book *Race Against the Machine*, they found alarming figures: 'In July of 2011, 25 months after the recession officially ended, the main US unemployment rate remained at 9.1%, less than 1 percentage point better than it was at its worst point' (2011, 2). They discovered that companies might have stopped shedding workers, but they didn't hire people. Analysing figures of the US Department of Commerce, they also found that investment in equipment and software had already returned to 95% of its historical peak (2011, 3). These numbers indicate clearly that the recession was only over for the machines: companies bought new equipment, but they didn't employ. Here, algorithms seem to level the skills middle-class societies

DOI: 10.1057/9781137373502

are built upon. An alarming development fortified by our archaic definition of skilled work and our antiquated discourse of the expert. As this
often blocks our discovery of new tasks and assignments, we should look
closer into the recent development that hit expert work.

It is a well-known fact that the exclusivity of the expert was an effect of a
former scarcity of knowledge typically for the printing age (Eisenstein 1979,
Bunz 2013). This has changed with digitalization; we now deal with a constant information overload. The formerly exclusive knowledge 'expertise'
has become abundant, often thanks to productive online collaborations
that have been enthusiastically described by Clay Shirky (2011). Today, the
'knowledge gained by repeated trials' to which the Latin word *experentia*
once referred to, can be downloaded from the internet including the five
most important facts of how to handle office hierarchies. As a result, the
authority of the expert comes under attack. Experts are swept away by the
ever-expanding wave of knowledge that unfolds with the internet. People
even begin to fear of drowning in information overload. In the wave of
algorithmically organized knowledge, new questions evolve for society:
Does the unlimited supply of knowledge overtake its demand? Already
in 2002, Scott Lash had detected the first reconfigurations of information.
Can knowledge still be of power in the age of its abundance?

One thing is certain: in the history of mankind, knowledge has been
closely linked to power and authority. Throughout his work the French
philosopher Michel Foucault has made us see innumerable and complex,
marvellous, and alarming ways, in which power structures and knowledge
intertwine: statistical knowledge puts governments in control, political
knowledge plays the imbalance of forces, scientific knowledge backs
up decisions of exclusion and inclusion, medical knowledge decides on
life, death, and insanity and so on (Foucault 1961, 1975, 2007). In short,
knowledge co-transforms the hierarchy of a society. It fuels the power
of the discourse: to a great extent this power of knowledge is imposed
upon us by experts; experts who take their authority from knowing all
the facts by being more exclusively linked to a discourse than others. As
the internet makes knowledge and expertise available, the authority of
our experts trembles. However, not only our elite wavers. We all do. As
seen above, we all became experts: today's working identity is based on
being educated, and job applications usually explain how one has gained
some special knowledge, which makes us perfect for a certain job. To
understand digitalization, we must learn how the field of knowledge
transforms with its algorithmic administration.

DOI: 10.1057/9781137373502

The transformation of expertise is nothing new: with the worldwide protests of 1968, institutional knowledge and the traditional concept of power is put under pressure to set race and class differences aside. In a postcolonial world, the hegemony of the expert follows a new narrative. Equal access to education becomes a central issue. Knowledge can be acquired by anyone who is willing to hit the books. For this, knowledge institutions are certainly of help. As a matter of fact, libraries are not only archives that manage our knowledge, but also machines that help to produce concentration; an important aspect that should not be forgotten despite the promises of online learning. Reading rooms isolate us in front of our books. As we are neither allowed to chat with our neighbours nor to pick up our phones, it is quite hard to get away from learning. Material books might be outdated in the future, but the ability to concentrate and with it its little helper, the library, isn't. This is the case despite the fact that we concentrate on different aspects of knowledge, because the old way of storing knowledge is made redundant by the internet. Specialist knowledge, once hard to find, is now relatively easy to get at. To sort through all this information, however, students acquire new reading skills: we now find 'hyper reading' a skill necessary to sort through mountains of texts, next to 'close reading' and 'symptomatic reading' as Katherine Hayles has pointed out in her far-sighted study (2012, 62). This transforms the field of knowledge, and with it the role of experts. Before, knowledge was buried in reference books solely available to the ones who studied them. Thus, the relation between a layman and an expert was asymmetric, the more so as experts tended to stick among themselves. With the rise of digitized knowledge, this relationship has profoundly changed.

Our health gives very good evidence of the social transformation that happens with digital knowledge: online we search for symptoms, and weigh up therapies. Concerned about the most precious thing we possess, our lives or the lives of our loved ones, we have started to reach out for expert knowledge accessible to us for the very first time. We post questions to a forum full of other patients, asking about the malfunctioning of body parts that would make us blush when mentioning them to a nurse. We look up medical terms and conditions on Wikipedia, and get our head around the details of a diagnosis. In peer-to-peer health care, we exchange detailed experiences with strangers, listen to their advice, and suggest tips on how to naturally balance the side effects of a drug. In short, we rebel against becoming a sheer carrier of an illness, an

DOI: 10.1057/9781137373502

object – and technology helps us to do so. Studies have shown that the doctor–patient relationship is deeply affected by its digitalization (Broom and Adams 2010). Some doctors point out that patients confuse their symptoms, and opt for the wrong treatment. Others welcome the new dialogue with a better-informed and less-inhibited patient, and approve the attempt to get at least a bit of control over a disease. As a matter of fact, self-diagnosis online is actively encouraged by the British National Health Service that asks you to 'Check your symptoms'. Planet body has even become a mobile phone application. We access it by 'Vision Tests', 'Dream Meanings', or 'Sex Facts', to name but a few of the most popular medical apps. We keep track of our 'Sleep Cycle', or keep a 'Headache Relief Diary'. To a certain extent one could say that playing doctor has successfully been transferred from kids to adults.

For doctors, this isn't all. As a matter of fact, their expert knowledge is under another attack. Thanks to the internet, the formerly exclusive expert knowledge is not only digitally available, but the size of medical knowledge has vastly expanded, too. Even if an expert will consult colleagues or tediously look up new facts, he can't know it all. As a result applications aren't just assisting the laymen but also the experts: like 'Epocrates' (2013), a medical phone application for professionals. Founded in 1998, the company announced already in 2000 the decision to deliver their knowledge directly on handheld devices, back then this was Palm. Ten years later, their aim was the same: to provide doctors with current drug disease and diagnosis information at the 'point of care', the patients. Making use of over 20,000 international statistical classifications of diseases, the app advises about risk factors, suggests the most important tests for a disease, plus further ones to be considered. Providing a high-resolution image library, it displays diseases with similar symptoms for a differential diagnosis and informs which drugs are available hereby giving access to a drug-interaction checker that enables one to ask for contraindication within different drugs, calculating the interference of about 30 at one time. It provides over 600 alternative herbal medicines, and allows filtering all drugs covered by the patient's insurance. It helps with a detector to find out what kind of pill has turned up, and delivers relevant medical news.

With all these features, the application Epocrates is a rather good example of the erosion of the classical expert's authority; for side effects simply consult your smartphone. Summarizing the points above, we find the expert at the following loss:

DOI: 10.1057/9781137373502

▸ Expert knowledge formerly difficult to obtain isn't exclusive anymore, but can be looked up online by everyone.
▸ Vast databases offer a knowledge way beyond everything the memory of an expert could possibly know, and makes it more likely that experts might miss something.
▸ Digital information constantly produces news, and facts change fast. This makes expert knowledge supposedly outdated and not accurate.

Discourse and distress

As the most important skill in our Western societies is expertise, algorithms aren't just intimidating our doctors, but all of us. Constantly we are seeing proof that we don't know enough anymore. Machines know better, faster, and more. Not only have the fields of knowledge become too vast for a human overview, also facts cannot be learned once and for all anymore. Change, once desired, has become a threat. We are in permanent need to update our knowledge. We can't keep pace. The pace is inhuman. Digitalization upsets us; we become insecure, and find ourselves unsettled and worried. We are at a loss. We wake up with the feeling that we need to work harder. We go to bed with the fact that we will never know enough. There will be some new information in the next days, hours, minutes, seconds, and it will come from London, New York, Shenzen, Tokyo, Gdansk, Berlin, or Bangalore. Better update. Our expertise is constantly threatened, which leaves us with the impression we cannot do our job. Our job security is at stake. It is of no wonder that the French sociologist Alain Ehrenberg speaks of our working environments as 'the antechamber of a nervous breakdown' (Ehrenberg 2009, 184). The fear of not being up to date is real, and it rose with the internet: being a niche product for decades, antipsychotic drugs became in this century the top-selling class of pharmaceutical, according to figures of the health agency IMS. By 2009 they were generating an annual revenue of about $14.6 billion, thereby even surpassing sales of heart-protective statins. After Western societies have managed successfully the threat of hunger, cold, and poor sanitation, fear has become the new misery of our societies (Robin 2004). And fear is closely related to our working environments.

DOI: 10.1057/9781137373502

This almighty fear seems to be triggered by the digital technology we all find ourselves working with everyday. Experts of digitalization indeed have warned us that something has gone wrong: they say that technology made us alone altogether, that the internet is moving us from the depths of thought to the shallows of distraction, and that we need to understand that we are not our gadgets (Turkle 2011; Carr 2010; Lanier 2011). But is this really true? Aren't we blaming technology for these problems a bit too easily? Does my mobile phone force me to be available after office hours, or is it my boss who expects me to be available? Has Facebook damaged my reputation, or is it the colleague who wants my job? Has an algorithm denied me the access to a reasonable insurance rate, or the board of directors whose criteria put profit before humanity? For sure, our societies are troubled by misery and fear. But it is the logic according to which we let things slide that is to blame for this, not the algorithms. Fighting the machines (or even breaking them) has already been proven useless – industrialization happened despite the Luddites.

As the impact of digitalization is comparable with the impact of industrialization, there are lessons to be learned. Contrary to the widely held opinion, in the beginning of the Industrial Revolution machines didn't replace the workers. It is true: much like the digitalization of knowledge today, the mechanization of work changed the logic of work, but it didn't dictate how rigid that logic had to be. Where did the rigid discipline that produced the worker as an appendage of the machine come from? English history knows how this realignment of work had happened. When the historical economist Polanyi researched the social and political upheavals in England during the rise of the market economy for his study *The Great Transformation* (1944), he already pointed it out: surely the machines changed the logic of work, but it was the people who interpreted this logic in such a drastic fashion.

Before the advent of machine labour, the labourer didn't depend on money alone. Family earnings acted as a kind of unemployment insurance (Polanyi 1944, 75, 96). The domestic industry was shaped by the facilities and amenities of a garden plot, a scrap of land, or grazing rights. Work wasn't an activity, but part of life itself. Parallel to the advent of the machine, however, enclosures of the common and consolidations into compact holdings had the effect that the weaving peasants lost their right to pasture their animals. Farming couldn't cushion poverty anymore. Instead, families needed money to live. From that moment on, it wasn't anymore the product that was carried to the point of sale. Instead of the

DOI: 10.1057/9781137373502

woven good, the weaver carried his or her body to the manufacturer, and work became a commodity. It was for sale. The role of labour and with it the life of the worker changed. Work now had a whole new meaning. It wasn't something that was embedded inextricably in everyday life anymore. It became a sphere of its own. The silent film 'Metropolis' of director Fritz Lang visualizes forcefully the brutality of the workers, who struggle to keep in time with the machines. But his film also makes apparent that this strict timing has been imposed upon them by the factory owner, and not by the machines – machines don't care if they run fast or stop to stretch their legs. The rules of the factories, which brutally diminished the personal freedom of the workers, were not given by the machines but by man. As the historians Alfred P. Wadsworth and Julia de Lacy Mann point out in their impressive study on *The Cotton Trade and Industrial Lancashire 1600–1780*:

> As industry came under closer capitalist control, and the numbers of the propertyless proletariat increased, the temper of employers set more firmly and consciously towards the imposition on their workers of the rigid discipline, economy of time, and 'enforced ascetisicsm'. (Wadsworth and de Lacy Mann 1931, 391)

It was the 'mental attitude' that the employers had towards their factory workers, it was the employers' 'eternal railing at the idleness of the working classes', that led to the imposition of a rigid misanthropic logic to the workers (Wadsworth and de Lacy Mann 1931, 391). While the machine surely changed the notion of work as it turned work into a commodity, the rigid discipline that was forced upon the worker did not originate in the machine but in the vision of their capitalistic employers. This vision turned human workers into a cheap commodity despicably expressed in the English writer Arthur Young's quote:

> Everyone but an idiot knows that the lower classes must be kept poor or they will never be industrious. (cited after Wadsworth and de Lacy Mann 1931, 389)

Consequential in the anti-machinery riots of 1779, it was not the machines in general which were condemned by the weavers, but only machines which were associated with social misery introduced by capitalistic conditions – Spinning Jennies that handled over 24 spindles, because those were 'unfair' and in capitalist hands (Wadsworth and de Lacy Mann 1931, 497). While stories of resentment against the new machines, stories of riots and attacks against factories seem to back up

DOI: 10.1057/9781137373502

the narration of man vs. machine, historical details reveal a different story. These early Luddites didn't fight the machines but their exploitation by a rigid capitalistic logic. Technology wasn't their enemy. On the contrary, the weavers themselves even pirated Kay's invention of the Flying Shuttle to enter the new inventions into possession, and not just in one occasion (Wadsworth and de Lacy Mann 1931, 465). Similar to the early ad campaigns of the music industry, which declared the copying of digitalized music as a criminal act, Kay reacted by placing ads in the newspaper to warn the weavers in Leeds of using the Flying Jenny without paying due to the patent; also he prosecuted them. All of this makes apparent: it wasn't the machine but the capitalistic logic that must be held responsible for the horrifying attitude towards industrial work and the worker, until the principle of social protection set in much later.

In recent political theories, this important differentiation between technology and the logic it is enfolded in often gets mixed up. In their influential study 'Empire', Negri and Hardt take up the baton from the Frankfurt School to focus if at all on the repressive sides of technology. Technology is addressed as an a-human other, automation and computerization is seen as repressive: 'Today we increasingly think like computers, while communication technologies and their model of interaction are becoming more and more central to laboring activities' (Negri and Hardt 2000, 291, also 267). Slavoj Žižek's *Living in the End Times* likewise deals with technology *en passant:* when provocatively describing capitalism as the true revolutionary, he names as an example for this how it has changed technology (Žižek 2010, 419). *The Soul at Work,* Franco Berardi's analysis of the dynamics of capital in its 'cognitive' phase, gives the topic finally the attention it deserves. As Berardi writes critiques of capitalism, however, he naturally focuses on technology in capitalistic usage, and writes that 'the invisible hand has been embedded in the global technology' (Berardi 2013, 25–26). Again this creates the impression of technology being entangled with a capitalistic essence, a story which can be challenged: having studied the ethics and aesthetics of hacking, Gabriella Coleman's book *Coding Freedom* (2013) has, for example, a very different story of technology to tell. In other words, the role of narration, that is how we address technology, is crucial (Weber 2005). 'The most powerful cause of alienation in the world of today is based on a misunderstanding of the machine', writes Simondon (1958, 11). Most certainly as long as we approach digitalization first and foremost with the question of profit, capital will emerge; and albeit it is easy to think 'profitable' is good, we

DOI: 10.1057/9781137373502

very well know capital doesn't automatically equate to a benefit to society. A society is something different than its economy, and that means we need to start demanding something different from digitalization.

The good news: there is hope that there is something else. Despite our worst fears, technology has been rather beneficial to our societies. Since the invention of the Flying Shuttle at the dawn of industrialization roughly 250 years ago, the improvement of living conditions in the Western world is impressive. For sure, the working conditions of industrialization were horrendous and technology has industrialized war. However, due to industrialization societies were also able to feed an increasing number of people, and experienced the growth of a population whose health has been made possible by progress in medicine and hygiene. It was the machines that produced the condition for a middle-class majority, which lives sheltered in warm or air-conditioned houses, enjoys education and a proper amount of leisure time, travels for holidays to foreign countries and has a fulfilling work life. Compared to the life of a weaver in the eighteenth century this is clearly an upgrade, and nobody will deny that a proper part of it we owe the machines. Luckily, there is no indication that in their attitude towards us, they have changed their beautifully passive minds; for minds they have, and now more than ever. Fearing for our jobs or clinging to antiquated concepts of knowledge, while not being able to stop technical progress is not an attractive option, but a miserable choice. Algorithms offer our societies chances, which we need to take or they will pass by. Therefore, it is important to understand what algorithms are about, what they demand from us, and how we, the experts, can make use of them. Answering the question of how contemporary knowledge changes with the rise of digital technology is a task for the humanities. This discipline, rich in expertise of the history of knowledge and the analysis of thought, is to be combined with the actual development of algorithms. For this, we need to jump right in the middle of things: what are the algorithms doing to the expert, and how can society benefit?

On a new accuracy of facts

Tasks for which you needed expertise have been outsourced to software, hence at first sight it seems as if applications steal the knowledge of us experts. In the past, genes have been designed in special labs, for

DOI: 10.1057/9781137373502

example. Today, everyone can calculate them on a phone: the biotechnology enterprise New England BioLab (NEB) Inc has programmed a small tool, which helps to handle deoxyribonucleic acid (DNA) by enabling you to find a matching restriction enzyme needed to cut DNA. The NEB application provides us with knowledge about the enzyme 'Earl'. We learn its sequence CTCTTCN^NNN_, its incubation temperature of 37°, and its inactivation temperature of 65°. If we find a digestive enzyme that fits, we could start genetic engineering. But can we really? While the expert knowledge lies digitalized at our fingertips, this doesn't turn us into molecular experts. Surely the app is rated useful by biologists, only we don't know what the app is doing. Helplessly we click through the details of these enzymes. Unless we are molecular experts, we can't assess the facts provided by the application. Here the digitalization of expert knowledge hits a wall – a useful collision which makes the shift of knowledge and its new borders apparent. While digitalization outsources knowledge formerly 'stored' in our experts, that doesn't mean everybody is able to handle it.

For sure, algorithms can sort digital data faster and more efficiently than humans, but the knowledge fields they make available need to be handled by experts. If algorithms are left alone, they might go wild. An example is algorithms that have collided at the stock market: on May 6, 2010 the Dow Jones plunged at the New York Stock Exchange by 1000 points in 20 minutes. The biggest one-day decline so far is known as the 'Flash Crash'. The reason was trading algorithms running wild as financial markets are more and more driven by software deciding when, where, and how to trade faster than humans punching orders into a keyboard. This ranges from automatic technical trading often done by hedge funds, to execution algorithms handling large financial volumes and breaking them up, to high-frequency trading that introduced a new liquidity to the market.

Things are speeding up by avoiding human intervention, but the downside is: the algorithms lack judgement. They have to be monitored – after the Flash Crash, the New York Stock Exchange fined Credit Suisse for failing adequately to 'supervise' an algorithm developed and run by one of the bank's subsidiaries. To this, the French philosopher Simondon would surely agree. Explicitly he sees a new linkage between man and machines: 'One could address what we have named the linkage between man and machine by saying that the human is responsible for the machines. This responsibility isn't the one of a producer, in the sense

DOI: 10.1057/9781137373502

of the produced thing which was created by him, but the one of a third, the witness of a difficulty that only he can solve, because only he can think it through' (Simondon 1958, 145).

We face this human responsibility towards the machine Simondon describes in the fact that an algorithm isn't neutral – its operation only seems more objective than a human. The filtering of information might be done automatically, but humans set the parameters of automation. Surely Google might argue in its company principles 'Ten things we know to be true' that they 'never manipulate rankings' and this is the reason that 'users trust their objectivity' (Google 2013). However, as it is made by man, it is programmed to act objective, and hereby follows a certain interest – in this case the interest of objectivity, for which Google even uses human raters.

While algorithms open up new fields of information, they still depend on human judgement and need experts to virtuously guide them through the new knowledge landscapes. The reason for this can be found turning to the *Critique of Judgment* of Immanuel Kant (1790). In the important and widely discussed paragraph §49 that Kant added very late when writing the book, he analyses the faculties of the mind that constitute a genius, which today helps us in understanding the role of an expert: in order to define truly creative work, Kant states the need of a 'free employment' of our 'cognitive faculties' 'without any constraint of rules' (Kant 1790, 146). To differ from imitation, the genius needs to be able to think freely, for only this 'reveals a new rule which could not have been inferred from any preceding principles or examples' (ibid.). While in the past, these deliberations described the work of a talented man, now they provide us with an approach to the work of human experts. This becomes fully apparent, when we apply the notion of 'free' to both, human expert and algorithms: here, the latter is by definition following specific instructions, in which a random factor is calculated in order to produce a creative effect; the human mind, on the other hand, produces a concept which can still be inspired by rules, but isn't obliged to any of them: it is free. And, with the help of algorithms it thinks free in a new way.

Today, we don't need experts anymore for just knowing the facts but for developing new rules. Leaving the opposition of man vs. machine behind, we can describe algorithms not as replacing our *work*, but as enhancing our *skills*. For this, an expert not only has to understand the new knowledge field but also how it is collected by algorithms: 'The

DOI: 10.1057/9781137373502

human' writes Simondon, 'comprehends machines; he has a role to play between machines rather than over and above them' (1958, 138). Following Simondon, we can say that the human needs to be with the machines, to look after them, guard them, and tune existing algorithms on our digital helpers, as algorithms too often and despite the obvious can't help themselves but follow the rule. This is already setting off a debate about the need of an algorithmic ethic, for example, in the field of organ transplantation (Quigley 2008; Verbeek 2005). Even here, algorithmic assistance is useful.

In general, algorithmic help tremendously unburdens the expert's brain, a principle used when we monitor content with a simple technique such as a Google Alert: if we don't want to miss any news about a competitor or a football player, we set up the service to alert us with an email. We disburden our brain from bothersome research by outsourcing our interest. Tasks that heavily rely on being up to date every second, on crunching vast information, or delivering a wide overview, tasks that involve filtering, sifting, and structuring information are wasted on a human brain and better optimized by algorithmic intelligence. Thus, regarding the expert we can conclude the following:

▸ Algorithms automatize tasks of the mind, but they don't replace the expert.
▸ Automated tasks need to be guarded and can only be assessed by experts with contextual knowledge.
▸ Algorithms always follow rules, while human experts have the cognitive faculty to think freely, thereby exploring and developing new rules.
▸ Algorithms unburden the mind, and can be used to explore new fields of knowledge.

Thanks to digitalization, we can actually move information mountains; only that we haven't made up our minds which ones we want to move. An interesting reaction: instead of being enthusiastic about the new possibilities of sifting through more knowledge than ever before, we have suspected them with Nicholas Carr (2008) of 'making us stupid'. After having clarified that the role of an expert has still a place, it is now time to understand where the hypothesis, technical knowledge makes us stupid, is coming from.

A first hint for this is found in an ancient argument concerning the nature of technology and its complicated relation to knowledge: While

DOI: 10.1057/9781137373502

science looks for knowledge proper, technology is generally considered to be after a less-pure endeavour: it is considered as applied knowledge or practical knowledge. This differentiation can be traced back all the way to Aristotle (2003), who described *episteme*: 'a demonstrative state' (19) in opposition to *techne*: 'concerned with production' (20), albeit a close reading like Richard Parry's (2008) reveals that he also mixed both concepts. Today, introductions to the philosophical concept of technology (Mitcham and Mackey 1972; Scharff and Dusek 2003; Parry 2008) often still refer to Aristotle. As the examples below show, again and again, science and technology have been understood as related to the troubled oppositional concept 'theory and practice', and over the years, this division has resonated in several philosophical approaches: for some, the field of technology is structured by a different logic than the field of science, which looks for investigation not for efficiency (Skolimowski 1966); for others, technology is described to be of different quality: it is a 'knowing how', not a 'knowing that' (Jarvie 1967, relating to Ryle 1949); concepts that can now be extended to another quality: 'knowing with'. However, while we follow the concept that technology is a knowledge of its own kind, we can obviously still suspect it of making us stupid. And this is an interesting aspect we need to further look into. Then the following becomes obvious: that we think of technology as a problem cannot be erased by thinking technology as knowledge. The problem is located somewhere else. Its origin can be found in the circumstance that we still approach technology as knowledge of a second-rate quality. By thinking it second rate – just practical – we introduce an opposition between what is good for us, and what is not so good for us. Clandestinely, the concept has lead to an oppositional thinking. With this, technology becomes quickly a knowledge that opposes the human culture – a notion explicitly repelled by Simondon: 'The opposition between the cultural and the technical … is wrong and has no foundation' (Simondon 1958, 9). In his essay on Simondon, Thomas LaMarre has described the implications of Simondon's strong statement further and it is worth reading LaMarre words in full extend:

> Technology is neither in opposition to biology, nor over and above the human body, but a continuation of it. Nor is technology situated as lesser to or below science, as a mere application of it, that is, as a lesser set of procedures than the 'higher' functions of the human mind. (LaMarre 2013, 82)

In other words, for Simondon, technology is no secondary knowledge. And that technology can't be categorized as such derives interestingly

DOI: 10.1057/9781137373502

enough from his concept of thought. As Simondon interprets Plato and explains the act of thinking in the 'Sophist', he describes it as follows: 'transporting an operation of thought [that has been] learned and tested with a particular known structure...onto another particular structure [that is] unknown and the object of inquiry' (Simondon 2005, 562; translation by Combes 2013, 9). Subject meets object via thought: in Simondon's reading, we find this addressed as 'an operation'. This operation is executed with a 'particular known structure' – here we can also recall again Phaedrus, a dialogue in which Plato explicitly states that dialectics is a tool that helps philosophers 'to speak and to think' (Plato 2005, 266b). However, thinking with a particular structure not only can be thinking with a technique such as dialectics, but it can also be thinking with a technology such as a calculator or an algorithm: 'knowing with'. As they fulfil the same role, this is the reason why technology is estranged to us, but still a continuation of the human thought, and not a knowledge of secondary rate.

Historically, the concept of 'knowing with' has also strong alliances. Encyclopaedias are one of them. Here, the classification of knowledge has been understood in positive terms and coined one of the great projects of enlightenment. When the first, the French encyclopaedia was published in 1751, it wasn't only the chief-editor Denis Diderot who was excited about the ambition to collect all the knowledge that 'before lied scattered over the face of the earth'. Many encyclopaedias all over the world followed, the *Encyclopaedia Britannica* – still running – being one of them. Google with the mission 'to organize the world's information and make it universally accessible and useful' (Google 2012) sets itself a similar goal, but isn't regarded as highly; not to speak of the information overload we blame on the internet. The fact that knowledge can now be organized without organizations, as media expert Clay Shirky has put it, isn't seen as the next step in gaining knowledge. Compared to the excitement about the encyclopaedia book series, we seem to fall back into old binary habits. To us, it seems as if the new technology is scattering what was once well and in order. Frequently the supposed overload leads to the fear of not knowing anymore what the facts really are – an interesting point, and true: with digitalization facts have changed. After discussing the role of the expert and our preconception of technology, the change of the concept of facts is my third and last point in this endeavour to understand why we believe digitalization is making us stupid. So how is digitalization changing the fact?

DOI: 10.1057/9781137373502

To be an expert meant in the pre-digital era to know the facts. Back then, to understand a field of knowledge you needed to make an investment, an effort. It meant to have a more detailed and deep knowledge of a field than others. It meant to know more facts, even the facts in the backwoods, where nearly no one ever came around. It meant a love for the obscure, rare, and absurd aspects of something. Because experts had a deeper and more detailed knowledge, they were able to find the right solutions. Superficial knowledge was opposed to expert knowledge: it was easy to get, vague, and led to the wrong solutions – something for the Jacks-of-all-trades, masters of none. When digitalization made widely available what has formerly been classified as expert knowledge, obscure, rare, and absurd aspects were suddenly to be found by everyone. Search algorithms crawl regularly the backwoods of the internet, and add what is found into their deep and detailed comprehensive index. Hence, due to digitalization knowledge is much easier to get; we simply do a quick search or browse some information. But while the 'here comes everything' of the encyclopaedia was greeted with delight, the 'here comes everybody' of the internet – to say it with the book by Clay Shirky (2008) – was grumbled about as if it meant an invasion of Jacks. Digitalization's achievement of opening vast areas of knowledge to everyone seemed to weaken the facts. The skill of the middle class, its expertise, came under attack. The rising availability of facts seems to shake up the validity of facts. However, this isn't the case. Instead, the condition of the digital fact is different, and this difference can be described as follows: The fact of our industrial past claimed truthfulness by being durable. This durability isn't compatible with the constantly changing knowledge landscape of digitalization. Algorithms are frequently updating the fact, with the outcome that it is being altered endlessly. While the digital fact has never been more accurate, it also has never been less durable.

Becoming a digital fact is functioning according to new and different rules. It is like the philosopher Alexander García Düttmann notes: It 'is simply not practicable to differentiate the question of what a fact is from the question of what the facts are' (Düttmann 2007, 76–77) – and now they are digital and functioning according to new conditions. Here lies the reason for our concern as well as the true challenge for us experts. It becomes obvious that the digital fact is relating to truth in a new and different way than the fact of the industrial age, for truth and facts aren't the same but share a rather complex relationship newly adjusted by technology. Instead of appreciating the fact's new accuracy, we have the

DOI: 10.1057/9781137373502

impression the ever-changing digital fact can't be true; truths don't alter as Hannah Arendt correctly pointed out (1967, 570). Obviously, we still judge the world according to the rules of an older discourse, the rules of the printing press that served us very well for so long; a printing press that wasn't demanding a fact to be updated as soon as possible in order to be more accurate.

With digitalization the logic of the fact becomes reorganized and the new condition confuses us and leaves us worried changing our orientation in the world. Wherever we look – whether to science, or politics, or economy – our Western societies function according to the logic of the fact. The new and different condition of a digital fact is a good example to make us see that we need to profoundly understand the new logic of the technology that surrounds us. Consequently, we need to tidy up our perspective on it. Our conception of technology has still its roots in industrialization, and the logic of this discourse shaped in the nineteenth century is casting its shadow on our view. But shadows can be illuminated. The next chapter will analyse our relationship with technology in order to make better use of this thing that has become our second nature.

Do you already depend on technology when you prefer to leave the house with an umbrella? Is it better to practice Californian ideology and believe in technology, or should we share Plato's critical concerns about it? And how do we iron out an ancient discourse that has troubled us for thousands of years?

DOI: 10.1057/9781137373502

3
The Second Nature

Abstract: *This chapter explores the role of technology as a second nature and contributes to discussions in philosophy of technology. In order to do this, it refutes the classic opposition of man and machine as well as the position of the human as a passive appendix to technology. Instead, it develops the concept of a 'distributed agency' by rereading the writings of Gilbert Simondon whereby two of his points are especially relevant: (1) human reality resides in machines as human actions fixed; (2) technology is always indeterminate as to function it needs to be open to an input. Using Google as an example to prove these points in praxis, it finds four disparate forces that generally unfold with technology: beside the logic of its technical functionality, there are the social effects of a technological achievement, its application as a technology of power, as well as a more general and slowly changing historical structure which is different for a tool, a machine, or an algorithm, as each one comes with a specific technical gesture which imposes a certain structure.*

Keywords: 'Philosophy of Technology', 'Social Technology', 'Technology of Power', 'Technical Gesture', 'Gilbert Simondon', Google, 'Long Tail'

Mercedes Bunz. *The Silent Revolution: How Digitalization Transforms Knowledge, Work, Journalism and Politics Without Making Too Much Noise.* Basingstoke: Palgrave Macmillan, 2014. DOI: 10.1057/9781137373502.

DOI: 10.1057/9781137373502

Once upon a time, we flew from the harsh environment of nature past the bonfire into our energy-saving insulated rooms. Here, sheltered from the rain, technology reversed roles with nature – there must have been a moment we didn't pay attention. Apart from catastrophic exceptions which usually prove the rule, we could say that nature might not be made but is mastered by man; while technology is entirely manmade however, following its own logic, digitalization is happening.

Digitalization is happening; we humans don't get to decide if knowledge will be automatized or not. The logic of technology, this is something philosophers for once agree upon, will always elude the men who made it. We need to accept that the thing we created has a life of its own, only this is not to be feared but to be understood as the physicist Marie Curie once put it. For there is more to come. Technology is happening, but this doesn't mean that the event of technology is already determined in detail, unable to be influenced by us. Unfortunately, we don't seem to have an idea what part we play in this progress. We live with misconceptions of technology, whether we fear or adore it, and we miss the point of playing our parts. In the advent of digitalization, for example, it has been a common concern that digital technology interrupts our life persistently. Its new way of communication was suspected of chipping away our concentration and stops us resting, as the clever computer scientist Jaron Lanier reminded us in a book with the brilliant title *You Are Not a Gadget* (2010). But when we feared that our new digital devices disrupt our lives for the worse, we found ourselves encircled by conditions that were actually not given: all digital gadgets provide a button to switch off their power. Consequently, it was not the gadget that was to blame, but a new, unhealthy work ethic that was imposed upon us humans: flexible capitalism has turned us into subjects always ready for use. That we didn't turn off our gadgets isn't the fault of technology rather than the nuisance of 'The new spirit of capitalism' (Boltanski and Chiapello 2005), which hides very well in technology. But technology shouldn't be mistaken for capitalism. For sure our gadgets, computer-phones, and other mobile devices have a major function in the new organization of labour (Berardi 2009, 89), but they are not dictating its organization in detail and according to an unhealthy capitalistic spirit. In a world with a technical reality, we need to learn how to differentiate between the technical possibilities given and our social interpretations of them.

This problem to think technology in different terms, however, is more severe than it might seem at first sight. Technology has been confronted

DOI: 10.1057/9781137373502

with objectionable allegations since quite some time. Already in the ancient world it gets accused of invading human expertise. Suspecting technology of enslaving humans started with a technique that was about to make an enormous difference: the technique of writing. In his dialogue *Phaedrus*, Plato made Socrates discuss his objections of external written characters with his disciples as they:

> will produce forgetfulness in the souls of those who have learned it, through lack of practice using their memory, as through reliance on writing they are reminded from outside by alien marks, not from within, themselves by themselves... To your students you give an appearance of wisdom, not the reality of it; thanks to you, they will hear many things without being taught them, and will appear to know much when for the most part they know nothing, and they will be difficult to get along with because they have acquired the appearance of wisdom instead of wisdom itself. (Plato 2005, 275a–b)

Isn't it astonishing? 2,000 years ago, that is long before Google, we humans had the same kind of fear we express when search became a new mode of knowing: we suspect the new technique being just a semblance of knowledge as it makes it shallow and impoverishes our senses. This problem in its persistence is impressively enlightening. Throughout history it sticks to the side of a technology that otherwise plays hard to get, because it is historically always changing: from tool to industrial complex, from the mechanical Stepped Reckoner to the digital telephone, from the jet fighter to the kitchen aid. But while technology shape-shifts as if it has plans to escape its own essence, its radical evolution is always haunted by the same spectre of impoverishment: it doesn't matter if it is the written word, microwave ovens, nuclear plants, tools, machines, or algorithms, technology will always threaten mankind, at best with the impoverishment of human skills, at worst with the extinction of the most basic one, to live. Therefore it is exactly at this point where we need to dig a little deeper. In view of the fact that technology is about to become our second nature, we need to understand this fundamental threat. What is at work in technology that had already freaked Plato out?

Interestingly, the concept of human as a passive appendix to technology is not only the case in our flourishing technological nightmares, which claim the despair of civilization. It can also be found when we praise technology as a helpful salvation. There is reason for this: as divergent as both approaches might seem, they address the same concept of technology. Indeed, Heidegger made this a claim when making

DOI: 10.1057/9781137373502

Hölderlin's quote central in thinking technology: 'where danger is/ grows the saving power also' (Heidegger 1954, 28). In both cases, men take the passive role, while technology is acting on man. If we look closer at the composition of the sweet song of technology that its futuristic fanboys sing, we find a fabulous salvation set to plug the leakage points of society. Technology solves our problems for us: when computers and the internet became mass media in the early 1990s, this approach rose. Coined 'Californian Ideology' (Barbrook and Cameron 1996), its visions were written by smart men such as the founder of Wired-magazine Louis Rossetto, the technology philosopher Arthur Kroker (1994), bestselling author and do-gooder Nicholas Negroponte (1995), sympathetic cyberpunk and science-fiction author Bruce Sterling, former publisher of The Whole Earth Catalogue and wise Christian Kevin Kelly (2010), and the transhumanist and business consultant Raymond Kurzweil (1999). Each proposed in their own way the same message: that digital technology will overhaul the body of society to replace the heteronomous mess lively politics is. Later, the filmmaker Adam Curtis would describe their cybernetic dream in his documentary 'All Watched Over by Machines of Loving Grace' (2011) as follows:

> at the heart of western political thought had always been a fear that if you allow individuals too much freedom you would get anarchy. But ever since the 1970s computer utopians in California believed that if human beings were linked by webs of computers then together they could create a new kind of order. It was a cybernetic dream, which said that the feedback of information between all the individuals connected as nodes in the network would work to create a self-stabilizing system. The world would be stable,... yet everyone would be completely free to follow their desires.

The idea that communication technology can deliver this dream had been put into dramatic demonstration as early as 1991. For this, hundreds of people gathered in a large dark room at the Las Vegas SIGGRAPH to find themselves in front of a giant screen, on each seat a small paddle. Soon they found out that each half of the audience controlled the bat on their side of the screen. If an individual held up red, a computer sensor picked it up and the bat went down a bit, and when it held up green, it went up. It was a game, 'Cinematrix Pong'. To play it, everybody had to collaborate in order to steer the bat. At first, when the individuals recognized themselves on the screen, the room cheered up. Then all went silent. Then the documentary report, which is part of Curtis film, shows a weird moment: an intense atmosphere arose as if a great leader

DOI: 10.1057/9781137373502

was about to give a speech at a party conference, but there was only technology.

The audience had quickly learned to jointly coordinate the mix between red and green paddles. Within the manageable setting of a game, this experiment proved that technology can empower individuals to make real-time well-informed individual decisions that also make sense in a group, at least as long as everybody wants to play according to the rules. However, it is a bit hasty to draw the conclusion; this proves a political framework can be replaced by technology. For one thing, political organizations have not been the megaphone for silent masses, and now that technology enables us to communicate and inform each other, we can get rid of it. Society doesn't behave like a well-balanced market; it needs a political balance. Friction and conflict are an essential part of our pluralistic societies (Mouffe 2000). For another thing, markets haven't always been so well balanced either, which is why we regulate them with rules. In fact, the market that we can find online is the opposite of 'well-balanced', a problem worth looking into.

In 2004, Chris Anderson, the American editor of the technology magazine *Wired* at that time, described a new economic model: 'The Long Tail' about which he later wrote a book (2006). His findings showed that online businesses such as Amazon, iTunes, or Netflix were making some money with hits, but they were making *more* money with what he called 'The Long Tail', niche products that don't sell very well. A lot of them. He described this new online market mechanism, and his conclusion is clear: in an online market, mass products were not the only economic force for businesses anymore. A study by a team at MIT led by Erik Brynjolfsson (2006) came to a similar conclusion. It sounded like good news: people were less hit centred than it had seemed. Apple, who had become a digital media store in 2003, announced one week later that 80% of their tracks had at least sold once. The economy, said Anderson, was shifting away from a focus on a relatively small number of 'hits' towards niches, towards the 'natural shape of demand' (2006, 53), which he called the 'market of multitudes' (5).

There were indeed several reasons for that shift: digitalization often leads to falling costs in production and distribution; compared to the narrow shelf in a shop, an online retailer can stock a massively expanded variety of products; and new filters helped driving down this Long Tail of variety (52–53). The remarkable development was in its early stages, but it sounded as if the distributed network had decentralized power.

DOI: 10.1057/9781137373502

Nonetheless Anderson was aware this technical market had some problems, for example that the 'Long Tail doesn't have a lobby, so all too often the Short Head is heard' (167). But his book gives the impression we can overcome this, when we leave our old scarcity thinking behind. However, the problems stayed. The reason for this is what Gilbert Ryle might have called an easily made 'category-mistake': Anderson and Brynjolfsson have indeed found a new business model. But what is good for businesses isn't necessarily good for people, or in this case for the producers. For sure, it was always hard to live from the money you make in a niche, and being able to distribute your product online opened a great new chance: it has never been easier for a niche product to find an audience. But this also caused a new problem. Being confronted with infinite choice, it became very hard to grab the attention of an audience. A few exceptional examples – artists that had made it from nowhere – were suddenly considered as validations and not as exceptions proving the rule. This fetishized anomaly camouflaged how the system had changed: for the producer, the digital business logic which sets in with the Long Tail makes grabbing the attention of the audience much harder.

In addition to this, the logic of businesses had changed: before the rise of the online market, the administration and distribution of each product absorbed a company's working power. To cover those costs, businesses tried to make sure each product sold as much as possible. In an online market, however, distribution comes cheap. The good thing: the market isn't focused on mainstream anymore, and the variety is bigger. The bad thing: it also doesn't care anymore if a product sells. The more products you offer in your online shop the better, and therefore businesses focus on scale instead of focusing on the product. The outcome: even a good product does not have a lot of chances on this scale-focused market. J. K. Rowling's book *Cuckoo's Calling* is a perfect example. After her success with the Harry Potter series, the bestselling author decided to publish under the pseudonym Robert Galbraith. The book got good reviews by acclaimed crime critics, but sold modestly; in the first three months 500 hardback copies. Then her real identity was leaked. What had sold 43 hardback copies the week before, suddenly sold 17,662 the week after the revelation, according to Nielsen BookScan data (BBC 2013a). A striking example which reveals: in a Long Tail economy, there are influential super hits followed by a long row of isolated single products that barely ever sell. These lonely products have no social impact and are replaceable. Unless you belong to the short successful head, you don't really

DOI: 10.1057/9781137373502

have a chance on this market. Having no middle ground doesn't matter for business, but it is a problem for the single product, hence for the individual producer. It is also a problem for a society.

In this situation, it is fatal if man finds himself as a passive appendage, instead of working with technology to cushion this effect. At the moment, technology is mainly used in a capitalistic logic, and as long as this is the case, technology is more inside than outside capitalism. The outcome is worrying. The statistical figure of the Long Tail shows more and more similarities with the trend of our distribution of income (OECD 2013). In the past ten years, the gap between the rich and the poor has widened. Is technology shaping society, or is it that we leave capitalism alone with it? In any case, our interpretations of technology – the hostile as well as the enthusiastic approach towards it – spare man from any technical responsibility. For sure, digitalization is happening, but as the philosopher Martin Heidegger once said: it needs man to make use of the essence of technology (1982, 39). Everything else is a misconception. That we do not make use of its essences, and don't show much of an effort in order to see through it either, is so much the worse as technology is by now everywhere, and from now on always will be.

An indifferent beast

In his remark, Heidegger spells out the two questions central for a philosophy of technology: What is technology's essence if there is one at all? And what is its relation to man? Luckily for us, an overview over the most important concepts of the latter question isn't that complicated. For centuries, philosophers have not given technology that much attention. The German scholar of enlightenment Johann Beckmann was the first to coin the term 'technology' studying mines, factories, and workshops to categorize them in his *Guide to technology* published in Göttingen (1777). The first book ever fully devoted to a *philosophy of technology*, however, wasn't published before 100 years later, 1877. Its author was Ernst Kapp, a German liberal who had fled to Texas. Inspired by Aristotle's idea of technique as an 'organon', which in Greek often means tool, he thought that technology was essentially built in the image of man. Thus, his compendium full of beautiful etchings begins with the analogy of hand and hammer, passing on from there to bones and bridges among others, and finally compares the network of blood vessels with a rail network. This

DOI: 10.1057/9781137373502

concept still leaves its trace in the contemporary reception of technology, for example when we mingle the internet and the brain. Subliminally the body–machine analogy is still at work.

With technology rising from tool to machine, man found himself as a sheer extension of the machine, an appendage – albeit being an appendage lead to quite different narrations. On the right wing, technology was understood as a helping tool or even a saviour, from the Italian Futurists (Marinetti 1909), who 'wanted to sing the man at the wheel, the ideal axis of which crosses the earth', to sociologist Arnold Gehlen (1957). For them tools and machines helped to overcome the deficient being that man always will be, and in order to confront the adversity of an always stronger nature, man reaches out for umbrellas, boats, floodgates, wellingtons, or wind turbines. While from the perspective of the sociologists of the Frankfurt School (Marcuse 1941; Habermas 1968), technology was seen as the opposite. Here, technological progress is threatening the free will of the individual and threatens mankind with the menace of technocracy. These rather different approaches to the relation of man and machine are an interesting occurrence. It becomes apparent that technology is of indecisive character as it gives way to quite divergent narrations – and this is the reason for the dialectical trouble Plato already mentioned.

Technology is obviously haunted by an ambivalence: it threatens to minimize our skills and determine our wills while also allowing us deficient beings to survive and even enjoy the comfort of a heated or cooled down house. As it has by now become our second nature, it is high time to bridge the gulf between these different perspectives of one and the same thing. For this, the concise writings of Gilbert Simondon are quite helpful.

It is likely that we owe Gilbert Simondon's innovative take on technology to the fact that he develops his approach side by side with his fundamental renewal of ontology. While his supplementary thesis 'On the mode of existence of technical objects' was published in the year of his disputation, 1958, his main thesis came much later and in two parts: 'The individual and its physico-biological genesis' (*L'individu et sa genèse physico-biologique*) in 1964 and 'Psychic and collective individuation' (*L'individuation psychique et collective*) in 1989. From the start, his philosophy was highly acknowledged even though not widely read. Gilles Deleuze named him as a major source of inspiration for his thinking. He enthusiastically reviewed the first part of his thesis (1966), and discussed

DOI: 10.1057/9781137373502

Simondon in 'The Logic of Sense' and 'Difference and Repetition'. Bruno Latour, Bernard Stiegler, and Paolo Virno, amongst others, refer to Simondon to develop specific thoughts with him further. In 1999 Muriel Combes' brilliantly subtle introduction *Gilbert Simondon and the Philosophy of the Transindividual* ushered new engagement, which was carried to English-speaking academics via new Simondon translations and essay collections such as *Gilbert Simondon – Being and Technology* (De Boever et al. 2013), which include contributions by feminist Elizabeth Grosz and social thinker Brian Massumi. Indeed thinking about 'being and technology' at the same time has led to quite a specific approach regarding a philosophy of technology, on which I would like to focus here shortly.

Simondon thinks technology and human reality *with* each other, and he does this in a very radical way. As already quoted, he strongly refutes first of all every opposition between man and technology as of 'no foundation'.

> The opposition...between man and machine is wrong and has no foundation. What underlies it is mere ignorance or resentment. It uses a mask of facile humanism to blind us to a reality that is full of human striving and rich in natural forces. This reality is the world of technical objects. (Simondon 1958, 9)

Master and servant, passive and active roles, give way to a network of relations between the two. Calling their relation a 'network', however, is only the start for his thinking. His plan is to consequently think their relations through. That their relation isn't oppositional, for example, doesn't mean it is balanced, friendly, or even seamless, and this is what excited Deleuze: Simondon's denial of an opposition leads neither to their synthesis, nor to sheer difference. Their relation is more than different. It is *disparate*.

> the machine is a stranger to us; it is a stranger in which what is human is locked in, unrecognized, materialized and enslaved, but human nonetheless. (9)

Simondon's surprising coup: in this estrangement, the relationship doesn't stop but starts. As in his other books, *disparation* is a recurrent reference for Simondon, and can be taken as the moment from which the connection rises. In other words, Simondon approaches the disparation of technology and human as their relation. They are *disparate*, but exist at the same level, and because they share a level, they can engage with each other. However, this engagement isn't easy. 'The relation between

DOI: 10.1057/9781137373502

the human individual and the technical individual is the most delicate to create' (119) – the centuries-old discourse of suspecting technology proves him right.

The choice of words Simondon uses is noticeable, in general. For one thing, his language performs his claim that we need to get over the opposition between man and machine. By letting them share the same name, 'individual', he sidesteps the concept of a human subject and technical object, which very easily reintroduces a certain distribution of roles. Instead, Simondon sees subject and object as two sides that emerge by a conjoint process, hence he can give them the same name. In addition, building his argument on the level of 'individuals' also prevents the assumption of any homogeneity of 'technology' or 'humanity'. Regarding technology, 'On the Mode of Existence of Technical Objects' argues instead along the lines of concrete technical inventions, it pictures technical engines and looks into air-cooled cylinders, it takes telephones apart to follow their development or categorizes triodes.

Simondon has reason for this. He is very aware that operating with broader characterizations such as 'human' or 'technology' introduces some essentiality often hard to notice, and he has a tendency to avoid this. Therefore, it's the inventor, or the engineer, the technician, or the user who engages with this machine, that tool – or that software. Their relation is one of engagement: humans, writes Simondon, are the 'interpreters of machines' (128). For this, they first have to understand their specific way of being: 'The technical life doesn't consist in steering the machines, but in existing on the same level to take on the same relation between them so they can be linked' (125). In thinking the 'technical individual', the machine gets constructed, regulated, operated, used, tested, and re-invented anew for 'The capacities of a machine are only those that have been placed there by its constructor: it unrolls its features as a substance develops its attributes' (125–126).

The humans understand the technical individual, but they still put their human reality in the machine. The machine, on the other hand, helps performing tasks whereby actions get fixed in a structure:

> Human reality resides in machines as human actions fixed and crystalized in functioning structures. (12)

With this Simondon manages to address the oppositional dilemma of technology from a new and quite different point of view: technology is human action set into a structure. By this, he claims a distributed agency.

DOI: 10.1057/9781137373502

While the opposition between man and machine melts into air, however, thinking technology can't stop here. We still come across the moment that already worried Plato for precisely in being at our service it is stealing our options. As it helpfully fixes human action it must hereby, of course, partly replace human skills, and this is perceived as a threat: technology impoverishes us. Thus, the cultural history of technology could be rewritten in an emotional version as a history of fear: from the worries of the Greeks that in reaching out for written texts instead of making our own experience, we become weak; to man being without free will and nothing but a sheer machine appendage; to Google making us stupid as online knowledge becomes nothing but shallow. In this impoverishment lies the reason why we fear technology, and why we find ourselves always afraid. However, it is a bit of a spurious argument, enough for sustaining through the centuries but only halfway true. The static side of the machine is only half of the story, here is the other half: as machines are used, they need to be able to process different inputs, and therefore necessarily must always be open to change. Tools, machines, gadgets, and apparatuses, they all must be adaptable to various situations and able to handle different input; this is also part of the essence of all technological things, systems and processes. This is the second important point that Simondon makes: 'The functioning of the machine conceals a certain margin of indetermination' (12).

For Simondon, technology is always open to different inputs: technology gets wielded or plied with; it is adapted to and used for different forms and situations; it processes different material or can be applied to different issues. Essentially technology must be partly indeterminate. To break this down in an example: Google, for example, is indeterminate at two different moments. Its usage: it doesn't decide what is looked for; and its findings: it delivers knowledge, but search engine optimizers are constantly pushing pages so that they are considered more relevant by Google's algorithms. No machine or algorithm comes as a closed box; all technology must necessarily be open to change. And how open technology is made is not only a service decision, but also a political decision; this is revealed by discussions ranging from Apple's iPhone to internet filters you need to opt out from.

The fixed task of the machine imposes a logic, but this logic isn't really a master. Technology per se is characterized by a certain openness and indetermination, and this means, we can always find some room to manoeuvre in the midst of our dilemma. The machine has no interest.

DOI: 10.1057/9781137373502

It doesn't will. The model 101 played by Arnold Schwarzenegger in the movie 'The Terminator' has a task and is consequently running focused through a supermarket – unlike us it doesn't suddenly reach out for the chocolate. Albeit technology is automatizing certain tasks, it isn't determining man. It also hosts a range of different narrations; upsetting the expert and scaring middle class with taking away their jobs is one of them, and just one – there are others and among them far more promising ones. Digitalization is happening, and instead of abdicating our responsibility, we must take our part more actively. But let us now that we have discussed the relation of technology and man not shy away from its other philosophical problem: what is its essence?

Google and the four aspects of technology

Technology is confusing. It is a network of meanings. To program the technical functionality of a digital device doesn't mean, for example, you are equally able to assess how the device will be utilized. Several philosophers of technology have made this important point, the reason why it is so difficult for us to 'think' technology: Langdon Winner when tracing automobiles from their making to traffic laws and urban transportation policies (1986, 9); Gilbert Simondon when describing the transversal ontology of tools to machines in the industrial era, in which the construction and the regulation of the machine become different from the machine's usage (Simondon 2012, 7); Martin Heidegger when following an airliner standing on a runway in the depths of language, demonstrating that technology is not equivalent to its essence (1954, 4 and 17). Understanding modern technology poses obviously the great difficulty of managing a variety of levels and moments that are just loosely bound together. Like Heidegger, Simondon looks at different 'entries of information' to an industrial machine. In great detail he points out invention, construction, first and ongoing usage to find these moments are not 'organically linked to and balanced out by the others' (Simondon 2012, 7). Which surely is the case: Being able to understand the technical performance of a steam locomotive didn't mean you were also able to predict in which way rail was about to revolutionize passenger transportation. Consequently, it wasn't an engineer who invented the package tour, but the Baptist missionary Thomas Cook. In 1841 he arranged a large group excursion, which combined the cost for a rail ticket with

DOI: 10.1057/9781137373502

food on the journey. Charging his customers one shilling, he started a new socio-cultural technology, package tourism (Brendon 1991). In the beginning, the new steam locomotive was at its centre, still package tourism can't be deduced from it. Their relation is *disparate*, which is why one also couldn't anticipate how 100 years later package tourism would become a political tool for the Nazi regime: 'strength through joy' was a large state-controlled organization making leisure activities available for the middle classes, in order to promote the German nation and pull the tourism industry out of its slump – by 1939 over 25 million people are said to have participated.

In examples such as these, it becomes apparent that the social aspect of a technology can't be deduced from its technical functionality, nor can they both determine, how they will be set up as a technology of power. Here, we come across a reason, why technology has its own logic. Technology has been treated as the paradigm of rationality, but it doesn't work according to our human rationality. It unfolds in *disparate* ways. It can't be predicted, or controlled. It can only be accompanied. To do this, the 'network reality' of technology (Simondon 2012, 11) has to be explored. Its four currently most influential nodes can be addressed as follows:

technical functionality	social technology
technology of power	technical gesture

The four aspects of technology

While all four aspects shape our understanding of a technology, they can't be deduced from each other. A confusingly loose relation is the case that was already recognized by Simondon. Therefore the social forces that enfold with technology are a rather complex matter. As the following example of Google makes apparent, depending on our focus – on a search's technical functionality, on search as a social technology that handles knowledge, or on its operation as a technology of international power – very different narrations come into view.

1. On the technical functionality of Google's search: If we focus on the technical functionality 'search', we see Google as a company that is managing huge amounts of data. In order to fulfil this task, it has developed some free services while it charges for others. Thus, its core search technologies are used for a variety of applications: next to search results it offers Google Maps, helps users searching Gmail to manage their

DOI: 10.1057/9781137373502

overflowing mail accounts, offers via its 2006 purchased video platform YouTube the possibility to search, find, watch, distribute short films and videos, and establishes with Google+ an alternative to the social platform Facebook. All these platforms, projects, and portals are then coated with contextual advertising. Google searches and matches contextual ads for you in its data set; a service that is also for rent to every other page in the World Wide Web.

To roughly understand what Google is doing in all these variations of search, we don't need to understand algorithms. It's enough to describe the algorithmic logic of search, which isn't very complicated. If we type a keyword in Google's search page, it is first sent off to Google computers, which hold an index of the World Wide Web. Keeping this index up to date, software robots or web crawlers permanently scan the internet. They collect copies of all the websites available to them, and send them to the Google servers, where the copies will be further analysed and indexed. This means, if you search with Google, its algorithms don't turn to the internet but simply look your search up on their own servers. In avoidance of getting swamped by the large quantity of online information, the copied webpages are archived and put into a neat index thereby scanning different fragments of a page: among them, for example, the web address, the headlines, the frequency of certain keywords, the captions and names of the pictures, pages that link to the site, or all other subpages that belong to the same address. All the information that provides orientation is looked at, in order to calculate which sites are relevant and should become part of the search results at the top of the result list. And as we humans are computable as well and predictably tend to look for the same keywords as our fellow humans, the results even don't need to be generated freshly each time from the index. Instead they are waiting for us ready for collection as Google has already found what we are looking for before we even have asked.

In order to know better, what its users are looking for, the search giant isn't only saving the information of websites, but also the search history of its users. This optimizes its results, as it provides the algorithms' orientation and helps them to grasp if you typed a keyword because you were looking for general information, or for pictures, videos, or actual news. To calculate the right answer from all those different options, the search algorithms are looking in detail at past searches of its users as well as checking different coordinates. When the algorithms register, for example, that in the last 15 minutes people have searched for a certain

DOI: 10.1057/9781137373502

term more often than usual, they deduce that something must have happened and deliver some news first. If it is a name like Darth Vader or Nosferatu usually related to a movie, they will also deliver you pictures or videos in the results.

By this time, Google has already given you a cultural identity, for in order to get a rough idea what a user might talk about, Google makes use of the IP-address your digital device needs in order to approach the internet. Search results are always filtered according to the nationality your IP-address belongs to, and this twists the results: If you type in 'orange' in Britain, the results deliver the homepage of a mobile network operator, the 1996 launched Orange price for fiction, a mountain bike brand, and a bit further down a link to the movie 'Clockwork Orange'. In France, Google's algorithms not only forget about the movie, but also assume you could search for the Provencal city named Orange, home for excellent wineries. In Turkey, on the other hand, the algorithms will deliver a slightly confused looking range of search results, as the colour there is named 'turuncu' and the term 'orange' doesn't really mean a thing. Here it becomes apparent that due to their technical functionality, algorithms operate of necessity selectively as they orientate themselves alongside certain categories. Thus, they will always only focus on a sub-territory of knowledge, and as algorithms have become the preferable way of getting knowledge beside books, it is by now essential to have a rough idea about how they are calculating results. Taking their knowledge wrongly at face value, we would lock ourselves in a comfortably pre-selected world that the American internet expert Eli Pariser calls 'The Filter Bubble' (2011).

2. On Google as a social technology: Looking at Google as a social technology, a different aspect comes into view: search changes how we know, and this leads to a fundamental social shift, an aspect that has been described in great detail in the second chapter of this book. To quickly sum it up again: from now on it is not important to know the facts, but to know *about* the facts. Today's experts grasp the consistency of a knowledge field and know about its continuous shift. Being able to navigate yourself through the knowledge landscapes of digitalization with search has become essential not only for work, but also for living. In this sense, the digital divide describes more than just an economic inequality. As search is a social technology, it is all the more problematic that at the beginning of the twenty-first century Google strongly dominates the search engine markets. In early 2012 Google had a global

DOI: 10.1057/9781137373502

search engine share of 66%, a figure that rises in the UK to 90%. At the heart of our digital societies, we find a quasi-monopoly. In most Western countries, 'to google' has become a transitive verb that means using a search engine.

3. On Google's services as a technology of power: After having discussed the logic of algorithmic search and visualized the upsetting of the expert, we now look at Google's power to move societies. Let us take Google's issue with China, for example. On January 12, 2010, the company announced on its blog 'A new approach to China'. In the past, it had agreed to censor its Chinese search results. Whenever someone searched for prohibited keywords of a blocked list, Google displayed at the bottom of the page: 'In accordance with local laws, regulations and policies, part of the search result is not shown'. After being confronted with a Chinese-originated hacking attack that tried to access the Gmail accounts of human rights activists, Google stopped censoring their search services and decided for a more confrontational tone. Redirecting its users from Google.cn to its Hong Kong branch Google.com.hk caused a political situation that had to be defused diplomatically. The White House said it was 'disappointed' that Google and the Chinese government were unable to reach an agreement 'that would allow Google to continue operating its search services', while the Chinese officials noted that the case should be handled 'according to the law' as Google had violated its written promise of filtering its searching service. To understand the technology of Google, it is also important to know about its political dimension.

4. On the technical gesture: The fourth aspect isn't easy to address, which is the reason why it has so far been standing in the corner. When technology behaves insubordinately, we experience a gesture inherent to a technical object or process, but differentiated from its technical functionality. Martin Heidegger observed it in his study of 'Being and Time' when he finds in the 'unusability' (1927, 103) of tools an obtrusive being of things; later he will remark in *The Question Concerning Technology* that 'technology is not equivalent to the essence of technology' (1954, 4). Technology is never simply a tool. The internet, for example, can be tamed and politically regulated, however, it can't be totally controlled. In China you could still use Google via Hong Kong or by fiddling with your network configuration and other associated technologies. Dealing more confrontationally with the 'Great Firewall of China', Google also replied with monitoring mainland China's service ability, which later turned into its world wide transparency report.

DOI: 10.1057/9781137373502

Nonetheless, the Chinese use the fast and therefore hard to control internet to post their views on websites, blogs or micro-blogging services, among them the writer Xuecun Murong and the conceptual artist Ai Weiwei. Xuecun Murong's debut work *Leave Me Alone: A Novel of Chengdu* (2009) is a nihilistic story of three young men describing the darker side of the Chinese boom. It was first published online with major success, which then brought the author the attention of publishers, and with it the obligation to compromise to censorship. He started to upload the censored parts online. Likewise Ai Weiwei, who used the internet to create a public he was hidden from. In the autumn of 2011 after being detained without charge for nearly three months, he received a punitive bill of $2.4 million in back taxes and large penalties. Using the fake name 'aihuzi', he was able to inform the Chinese public on the micro blogging site Weibo, and within days 30,000 people got in touch and loaned him $ 1.42 million which allowed him to transfer the money to the Chinese administration – a partial win. Using technology, both could escape the official line as technology is informed by, but not identical with, a society; there obviously is a different force at work which opens the intermediate space which was used by these artists.

That technology isn't identical with a society has often been noticed. Walter Benjamin wrote that technology is a phenomenon with a certain functional character, which it imposes on society (1936, 490). Corlann Gee Bush (1983) also 'unthinks' the notion that technologies are merely tools, asserting that their change stimulates social change. As technology informs a society, a technical gesture reveals itself, and this gesture exposes the force of the technology we live with. This force has been described differently: Bruno Latour (1999, 187 and 210) finds an 'activity of techniques'. Don Ihde (1979, 1990) concedes that technology has a certain directionality, which he calls 'technological intentionality'. Langdon Winner (1986, 6–7) notices beside the use of new technology 'powerful forces', which have a new 'pattern taking shape'. Peter-Paul Verbeek (2005) enquires 'what things do' and states that technologies actively shape the relation between human beings and their world. Hans Blumenberg (2009) discovers next to the spirits that create technology, a spirit that hereby is created and demands an intellectual history of it. Nigel Thrift (2004) writes about a 'technological unconscious' that is detectable in the technical process. Friedrich Kittler (2009) tracks down the technical Apriori in the humanities and unveils the effect of media ontologies on thinking. Gilbert Simondon

DOI: 10.1057/9781137373502

describes these activities as evolutive chains that create technical realities (1958, 65), but also finds a 'latent power of universality' that delivers schemas of intelligibility (2012, 1).

These philosophers and thinkers all strive after something that can be coined 'the technical gesture', a structure or 'schema' inherent in technology and changing with each new technical revolution. This gesture enfolds certain social forces. Industrialization, for example, is based on the construction of systems for which the process of standardization is essential. The digital, on the other hand, has a more disruptive and fragmented side so that flexibility is a far more important aspect to it than rigid norms. Such tendencies can be addressed in a similar way to Ferdinand Braudel's focus on the shift of long-term historical structures besides short-term historic events. Even though technology makes certain gestures, there is no technical determinism. There are different reasons for this: (1) There are *different gestures* over time. This shows (2) the logic of technology is essentially *disparate*. It reveals evolutionary jumps, from which the process takes off in another direction – in detail Simondon describes the 'rhythm of technical process' (1958, 37), its 'evolutive chains' (65) and the 'law of relaxation', which he also calls a 'law of serrated evolution' (67). This serrated form might also be explained by the circumstance that the different aspects of technology – social functionality, social technology, technology of power, technical gesture – cause technology to diverge. (3) A technical gesture might have its disparate logic, but this logic doesn't follow a specific interest and doesn't have a will. Instead, the concretization of this logic depends on how we make use of them; a point that often seems overlooked in the digital era. Instead of exploring the potential of a new technological logic for our societies, the focus lies far too often on shiny gadgets pleasing as they are.

Technology, however, changes what being in the world is in a fundamental philosophical as well as in a political way. Society shifts as we gather around machines in new ways that connect us and another differently and according to new patterns: we are different in the world and amongst each other. We restructure. Simondon thought it a fundamental problem that we address the technical object as a closed machine (1958, 145), which he criticized: 'Culture doesn't understand the machine. It is inadequate to the technical reality, as it considers the machine as a closed box, and its function mechanical like an iterative stereotype' (1958, 145–146). Of course, the same holds true today for algorithms. Instead of ignoring technology, he proposed a 'social relationship' with

DOI: 10.1057/9781137373502

it (1958, 88): working with each other's capacities. From this perspective, it is very interesting to show that our questioning of technology (and our social relationship to it) has become worse over time. Today, we mostly ask technology for profitable business, but not for a better society. In our past, the emancipatory potential of technology has been an important subject. As part of politics it has been described by the likes of Marx, Bertolt Brecht, or Walter Benjamin, for example, for whom technology opened up a new social potential: 'the revolutionary work of this hour is not conflict, not civil war, but canal construction, electrification, and factory building. The revolutionary nature of true technology is emphasized ever more clearly' (Benjamin 1927, 45). Rather than abolishing industrialization, these thinkers created an alternative political plan for it. And it wasn't only them. In former times, politicians of all range have understood the social interpretation of technology as a political task, among others Eisenhower and Harold Wilson have addressed the political force of technology.

After the launch of the Soviet Sputnik in 1957, US President Dwight Eisenhower was confronted with the political role of technology as this had set the US into a panic. Generously funding technological research, he planned to re-assure the nation. The money was, for example, invested in the newly founded Advanced Research Projects Agency, which later created the computer network Arpanet, a predecessor of the internet (Divine 1993, 19 and 125). Additionally the National Defence Education Act invested millions of dollars into scientific education in schools and universities looking for more talents from all classes to attend college. The prime minister of the United Kingdom Harold Wilson was also quite clear about the necessity to steer technology in order that it serves society. At the Labour conference in 1963 he proclaimed that Britain 'is going to be forged' in 'the white heat of this revolution', and 'only if technological progress becomes part of our national planning can that progress be connected to national ends' (Wilson 1964, 18 and 27). This approach towards technology has been lost. When US President Obama again invoked a 'Sputnik moment' in 2011, it wasn't about the governance of technology anymore. His words didn't ask for a technology to be shaped socially. It sounded as if technology defies any influence. 'The rules have changed. In a single generation, revolutions in technology have transformed the way we live, work and do business' (Obama 2011). It seems that ensuring a distance between man and technology is the ideology of our time.

DOI: 10.1057/9781137373502

While in our past, industrialization was philosophically explored and questioned for its best social use, our demanding attitude towards digitalization has been comparatively reserved – a point flagged up in their *Evil Media Studies* by Matthew Fuller and Andrew Goffey (2013). Albeit the impact of digitalization is often assumed to be as deep as the one of industrialization, we are not debating the potential it offers our societies enough. In the meantime, a silent revolution has happened, that fundamentally changed the ground on which our societies stand: the public, a mass of algorithms.

Does each medium organize public differently, or do they have something in common? Is digitalization splintering the fourth estate, or is the fragmentation of journalism at the heart of a pluralistic democracy? And will journalistic ethic get afraid on the internet, or has it toughened up already?

DOI: 10.1057/9781137373502

4

On the Production of Crowds

Abstract: *This chapter contributes to sociology of media as it looks into how digital technology has changed a public sphere which is now – thanks to Twitter, Facebook, YouTube, and blogs – created with the help of algorithms. In order to do this, the chapter discusses the role of the digital public by looking at examples like the reporting of news on Twitter, or the death of the British newspaper vendor Ian Tomlinson which could be solved with the help of digital recordings. Adding Hannah Arendt's description of the public to Jürgen Habermas's famous definition of 'the public sphere', the chapter finds that there is a digital public, when something becomes* potentially accessible *for everybody, and there is a journalistic public, when something becomes* potentially accessible *but also is* relevant *for all at the same time. Finally, it discusses the digitalization of the press which gave rise to a broader reach, new financial concepts, and new ways of reporting.*

Keywords: 'public sphere', 'Transformation of the Public Sphere', 'Jürgen Habermas's, journalism, newspapers, 'history of journalism', 'digital journalism', 'Hannah Arendt', 'digital reporting'

Mercedes Bunz. *The Silent Revolution: How Digitalization Transforms Knowledge, Work, Journalism and Politics Without Making Too Much Noise.* Basingstoke: Palgrave Macmillan, 2014. DOI: 10.1057/9781137373502.

Once upon a time, democracy emerged from pieces of broken pottery and small coloured stones, white for yes and black for no. The Athenian assembly of the people, the 'ecclesia', used them to express their vote, when a show of hands became impossible to count. At least 6,000 full citizens needed to take part, and to get the opinion of such a huge crowd required tools. From the beginning, democracy is inseparable from technology. It is technology which helps to organize our communication, and therefore our society: from the stones and shards of the Athenian city state to the eighteenth-century, book-driven 'republic of letters'; from the newspaper-informed democratic 'nation of readers' to the election debates on television; finally, to the internet. Once we become too many to show our hands orderly on a marketplace, we rely on technology. With digitalization the ears that once listened to the debates, and the hands that were raised to communicate with the leaders, get their news online, and type their opinion into a keyboard. As each technology leaves its marks on society, how is digitalization transforming the democratic public? Let us start with a closer look at the kind of crowd that can be created by digital technology, and compare it to the public in the era of the printing press created by newspapers. What is the technological condition of the public in the digital era?

First of all, political leaders don't rely anymore on the press in order to interact with the public in the digital era. The opinion of the people – once gathered by reporters and summed up in an article to be read by the decision makers the next morning – can now be communicated directly using the internet. While it is well known that prime ministers, presidents, and of course dictators eagerly fill their social media feeds, we often miss that governments don't need a report anymore to learn about public opinion either. Governments can make use of the internet, and gather public opinion directly of which the project 'Opinion Space' is an early example. In March 2010, the US State Department launched this project on its website. Its aim was to openly debate perspectives on US foreign policy; to gather public opinion, as well as to allow people to participate. Their first question: 'If you met the U.S. Secretary of State Hillary Clinton, what issue would you tell her about, why is it important to you, and what specific suggestions do you have for addressing it?' Over 4,000 participants from Mali to Norway discussed the range of foreign policy issues on the State Department's website. Climate Change, China and the world, single-entry visa for Iranian students, women's education, global peace, and Israel were central issues. This time, the people's

DOI: 10.1057/9781137373502

opinion wasn't evaluated using stones and shards, but by algorithms that visualized their diversity by mapping public opinion.

The project, which secretary of state Hillary Clinton called an example of twenty-first century statecraft (US Department of State 2010), was developed by the Center of New Media at the University of California with the aim of widening access to politics. Interestingly its approach also actively shapes the public opinion: to depolarize discussions, the questionnaire doesn't simply ask you to click 'yes' or 'no' in its digital survey. Instead, participants use sliders to 'agree more' or 'agree less' with a statement, by which Opinion Space aimed to open up debates among participants. In order to find a way out of obstinate oppositions, it tried an approach that sets itself apart from our industrial past, in which the public from press to parliament was organized according to the dialectical positions of left wing vs. right wing. The new approach made Opinion Space an interesting experiment, although despite the praise from Clinton it proved to be just that. Even though it was featured on the official website of the US State Department, it has never gained enough users to have a real impact, due partly to the fact that the State Department didn't embrace the digital approach fully enough. It didn't remove technological hurdles confronting users, and without constant cultivation and service, algorithms quickly feel like ruins of a deserted city. Opinion Space's basic concept, however, was exemplary. Nearly at the same time in May 2010 *The New York Times*'s multimedia editors Jon Huang and Aron Pilhofer would adopt a similar approach to depict public opinion. In the digital age, the opinion of the public becomes a visual pattern, in which no individual loses his or her voice. Digital technology with its sorting algorithms had changed the form and concept of the public.

The relation between the public and technology wasn't always so evident. When the sociologist Habermas wrote his account of the transformation of the public sphere (1962), he focused mostly on how laws and censorship, stamp acts and libel acts formed and controlled the army of readers. Habermas doesn't write about 'technique' in a technological sense, instead he discusses the technique of law and of public relations (1962, 23 and 193). His description of how mass media develops in the US, for example, is not driven by technology but by forms of content. The circulation rises, when newspapers pick up the repertoire from the weekly press to include cartoons, news pictures, and human interest stories: 'the weekend press and illustrated magazines were the pacesetters for boulevard papers proper'

DOI: 10.1057/9781137373502

(1962, 168). The commercialization of participation also had economical reasons, but its technological condition is absent. This is quite astonishing for a thinker who would publish the vibrant essay 'Technology and Science as Ideology' (1968) shortly after, although one has to admit, that the essay positions technology as rather passive. For Habermas, there seems to be no difference between technology and the economic–industrial apparatus making use of it. Informed by the technical reality of today, however, one would also say that for a reading public to establish itself, it needs a machine that produces a platform for this public. It needed a newspaper and its printing press. Today, one would place the study of the historian Elizabeth Eisenstein *The Printing Press as an Agent of Change* (1979) right next to Habermas's work.

Algorithms transform this public sphere anew. They change the communication between politicians and population and allow more differentiated ways of communication: an 'Interface Effect' as Alexander Galloway (2012) coins this. Technical means, design and politics are becoming intertwined, and the technical aspect of communication isn't a neutral force. Langdon Winner goes so far as to describe this as 'technological politics' (1986, 21). Like most other scholars, he agrees that the relation of technology and politics is a complex matter: one could say that technology doesn't determine the social conditions, but it favours specific political potentials and forms. This chapter will now look further into this with a focus on algorithms and the printing press as a social technology.

It is well known that what was once called the 'army of readers' started to conquer new territories: when Facebook was floated on the stock exchange in 2012, the platform had 845 million users making it metaphorically 'one of the largest countries in the world'. If we define a society in contrast to a community as something that binds people together through rather loose ties, one could say there was a new and additional society emerging. This time, their ties were not political but technical, which, by the way, is not without historical precedent. Facebook isn't the first country without territory (Bunz 2012). It was newspapers, which produced a crowd that 'does not have to assemble', as the philosopher Elias Canetti (1960, 52) noted in his book *Crowds and Power*. And with the introduction of the steam-powered printing press, technical advances allowed them for the first time to assemble not only daily, but also in vast numbers.

In Europe *The Times* is the pioneer of the trade. In 1814, its publisher John Walters II bought two new steam-powered presses. They had been

DOI: 10.1057/9781137373502

invented by the German printer Friedrich Koenig and made use of a revolving cylinder to speed up production up to 1,100 copies an hour. The first issue of *The Times* to be printed with these new presses was published on November 29, 1814. Now the masses could be reached faster than ever before. One could say that the revolution of the printing technology gave rise to the modern crowd: being able to reproduce words with such speed and in such great numbers meant that news became shared knowledge. The daily press pushed them to the same level of information thereby establishing between them a virtual connection. While the working conditions of industrialization tore families apart, the steam-powered printing press reintroduced peoples' connections on a different level: they read about the same. There was a steep rise in circulation: in 1817 *The Times* sold 7,000 copies daily, and in 1855 circulation was already up to 60,000 as the stamp act, Britain's so-called tax on knowledge, came to an end. Newspapers became cheaper, freed from paying the tax levied on legal documents. Around 1870 the *Daily Telegraph* reached 200,000 readers and claimed to have the largest circulation in the world. Finally, the idea that it is relevant to explain the 'news for everybody' was emphasized with the launch of the *Daily Mail*. The first issue, published on May 4, 1896, sold no fewer than 397,215 copies (Herd 1952, 130, 153, 166). Mass medium and the masses had finally met.

The publishing society

As the acceleration of the masses quickened, the nineteenth century experienced the rise of a new Leviathan, which would have caused the political philosopher Thomas Hobbes to rub his eyes in disbelief. In the political theory he had published in 1651, a social contract formed a people. It was put into play by a legitimate government, which created the social body of a nation. With the steam-powered printing press, a second body of a people came into being and started to speak: daily newspapers summoned the masses. For this, the newspapers also introduced editorial innovations: in 1817, the 32-year-old liberal Thomas Barnes was appointed as *The Times* new editor. He transformed the paper into the first powerful independent journal far ahead of its European contemporaries. *The Times* became an interpreter of public opinion. It established a network of correspondents throughout the country, and even collects information from people of different classes

DOI: 10.1057/9781137373502

(Herd 1952, 130). For nearly 200 years it was independent media that gave public its eyes, ears, and voice.

In the era of digitalization this would change in two very different directions. Driven by technical doability, the eyes and ears of the public have also started to record the private sphere as algorithmic-driven communication blurs the border of public and private. While it would go beyond the scope of this book to track down this change – Raymond Wacks (2010, 2013) and Jeff Jarvis (2011) have both thoroughly done this in profoundly different perspectives –, I would like to briefly mention one important point: Before digitalization, public and private communications used different communication channels: public communication with the aim of its visibility and its wide distribution, private communication shielded by a room, an envelope, or a direct line. Now both communications are based on algorithms, which come with a new technical functionality: they send communication by copying a message. This makes it not only easy to assess the message by its metadata, it also allows storing and looking into it without anybody noticing. Deep packet inscription is used by service providers and governments not only for internet management, but also for censorship. The US and other Western governments have also introduced a surveillance system on the basis of broad data collection. Seduced by a technical doability, governments have diminished privacy, and the right to privacy became a public concern. On the other hand, algorithms also gave the public a much louder voice. Their technical functionality introduced a new accessibility, and based on this the public started to publish their opinion directly on blogs, and platforms such as Twitter or Facebook, which began to handle over a billion messages daily. Powered by the algorithms of digital media, people reported the world around them, and it didn't take long for this new public to be the first to break important news. On January 15, 2009 a US Airways flight from New York's LaGuardia Airport bound for Charlotte, NC with 155 people aboard came into trouble after takeoff. It was forced to make an emergency landing on the icy Hudson River, where all passengers could get off safely. The news broke on Twitter, when user Janis Krums posted a picture of the plane on the river with the message:

> http://twitpic.com/135xa – There's a plane in the Hudson. I'm on the ferry going to pick up the people. Crazy.

The triumvirate of television, radio, and the press had been challenged by a fourth medium, the internet. Here, news could be made by everyone. The public sphere had been transformed again.

DOI: 10.1057/9781137373502

When Jürgen Habermas sketched the last structural transformation of the public sphere in 1962, he described a bourgeois public sphere that arose in the Early Modern Age to take its place beside the representational public of the court, which in most countries it later replaced. After the representational public of parliament, a new public arose when a 'sphere of private people come together as a public' (Habermas 1962, 27). Habermas interpreted this as a democratic group of voices commenting, correcting, and controlling the social contract. For centuries, journalists represented these voices until right next to the journalistic public a digital one emerged. Of course, this splintering of the fourth estate (Rusbridger 2010) caused deep social discontent, for in the political system of democratic societies, the journalistic public plays an essential part. Free and independent journalism is at the heart of the political system of a democracy. As the Founding Father and third president of the United States, Thomas Jefferson, once put it: 'were it left to me to decide whether we should have a government without newspapers, or newspapers without government, I should not hesitate a moment to prefer the latter' (Jefferson 1787). Jefferson, who got extremely worked up about newspapers when they published untruths, had a good reason for holding journalism in such high esteem. In our democracies, journalism provides a people with the information and facts they need to make an informed free choice on an election day, apart from keeping a check on those in power. If the system is spoiled, the public worries – the News International phone hacking scandal was followed by a judicial public inquiry such as the Leveson Inquiry (2011–2012), installed to look into the culture, practices, and ethics of the British press. As producing journalism – reporting – plays a central role for our political system, it is based on an explicit code of ethics: reporting must be devoted to accuracy, objectivity, impartiality, fairness and public accountability as well as being transparent about a potential conflict of interests. 'There can be no higher law in journalism than to tell the truth and shame the devil', the Pulitzer Price winner Walter Lippmann once wrote (Lippmann 1920, 13). To a certain extent we can say that it is in journalism where our secular societies embed their truths. In effect, Lippmann noticed that the relationship between readers and journalistic media is 'an anomaly of our civilization', as journalism is 'ethically...judged as if it were a church' (ibid.).

With the rise of a digital public this 'church' comes under pressure: journalism has to give up its exclusive role as the gatekeeper of

DOI: 10.1057/9781137373502

public information. Its power of ultimate opinion is questioned. The sheer amount of content published since the rise of social media makes it apparent that journalism isn't the only centre of public information anymore. Through digital media, a structural transformation of the public sphere has happened. From this transformation, a publishing society emerged: on an average Tuesday in June 2011 within 10 seconds, 106 blog posts were published, 6 hours of video content were uploaded on YouTube, 86,768 comments were made on the social network Facebook, and 10,625 tweets were sent on the micro-blogging platform Twitter, to name but a few digital activities calculated via live statistics of the media expert Gary Haynes. In the past, journalists smoked too many cigarettes, reported the news, and wrote up stories of public interest. They investigated facts and gathered information that was then published by a media house, which distributed the news to the masses. By the turn of the century, public smoking was banned and everyone could write up stories to distribute them to the masses him or herself.

However, the new digital public also enriched journalism. When digital technology was advanced enough to turn our constant companion, the mobile phone, into a proper recording and publishing device complete with a camera, the former passive consumer of news became a journalistic ally. Equipped with recording devices they were able to gather further source material. From now on, many events were accompanied by a 'distributed recording'. One of the first moments, when this distributed recording changed a journalist's ability to go after truth, was witnessed by the investigative reporter of *The Guardian*, Paul Lewis. Lewis tried to clarify the circumstances of the death of the English newspaper vendor Ian Tomlinson in the City of London during the 2009 G-20 summit protests. Officially, it was claimed that Tomlinson had met his death through natural causes. Then *The Guardian* obtained footage shot by an investment fund manager from New York, who was in London on business. His mobile phone recording suggested a different story: one could see a police officer, who seemed to push Tomlinson causing him to fall. Lewis started to scan pictures from protesters uploaded on the online-picture platform Flickr. Further videos, two of them filmed by bystanders, emerged. The material helped the journalist with gathering clues. The case, which was already set to close, had to be left open for further clarifications. The different angles of the videos indicate that the officer hits Tomlinson with his baton on the legs. The newspaper vendor falls and hits the pavement. A second post-mortem examination notes that Tomlinson died from internal bleeding and not by

DOI: 10.1057/9781137373502

natural causes. The British police had a scandal, and the truth wouldn't have been revealed without the videos shot by the bystanders.

Here we experience a new phenomenon, the *distributed recording of an event*. Due to our ubiquitous digital cameras, we are now more than a witness to what we have seen. In addition to giving evidence of what we have sensed, we can consult our mobile devices to see if we have filmed something that had escaped our notice. Our digital devices have become a second witness, a condition already anticipated in Michelangelo Antonioni's film 'Blow Up': A photographer strolls through London's Maryon Park taking pictures of a pair of lovers. Back in his studio, he discerns in the gritty grey of one of his pictures a person holding a gun and an inanimate body. He, or rather his camera, had been witness to a crime. Carrying a camera was still the exception, when Antonioni's film was released in 1966. Of course, in the digital era this changes. Ever after digital assistants help the users to upload and publish the material online, recorded material has additionally become accessible. Now simple technical processes allow on-the-go publishing as well as the gathering of a group of friends, or followers, or subscribers to the feed of a blog, or video channel – a structure generally referred to as many-to-many communication.

Back in the era of industrialization, the structure of public communication was shaped in the form of one-to-many, with journalists acting as valuable gatekeepers to the public and listening to the many in order to give them a voice. Then digitalization established a new publishing paradigm. Powered by the advent of digital tools in 1999 blogging gained popularity to finally become mainstream after September 11, 2001, when the first how-to manuals appeared. Soon blogs didn't make it necessary anymore to understand the language of webpages ('html') or to rent space on a server. Thanks to blogging platforms one can choose a name and a prefabricated design for free, and is ready to publish. The media theorist Geert Lovink notices that a 'massification of the internet' (2007, xxiii) sets in, and Facebook, Twitter, and other micro-blogging platforms soon take this to the next level. Now it wasn't even necessary anymore to write a complete text; simply posting a status about how you are doing was enough to go public: hello masses! The public is struck by a structural transformation, but it isn't the only one. Digitalization also opens a new phase in the thinking of technology.

In the industrial era, technology was often discussed as setting the capitalistic framework between the worker and the machine. Interestingly, the French philosopher Gilbert Simondon, who has been broadly introduced

DOI: 10.1057/9781137373502

in Chapter 3, insisted on a different perspective: technology could not be addressed as a simple support for labour. Instead, he saw the rise of a 'technical reality' (Simondon 1958, 146) made of human reality residing in machines. For him, capitalism and technology aren't identical. This is why the Italian Marxist, Paolo Virno concludes when reading Simondon: 'The machine gives an external appearance to what is collective' (2006, 36). Surely, our social organization can't be directly deduced from technology or vice versa. However, by technology giving the appearance, the social condition and the technical condition become fundamentally linked. In the era of digitalization, the link between a social organization and technology reads as follows: everything that is organized has a pattern and a structure. To form this pattern, or structure, or hold on to a certain pattern it requires communication, and communication is based on a technical element. A crowd or an individual is never simply there. Connections and distances are constantly communicated, negotiated, acknowledged, or denied: this is the work of a society, a work done with the help of a symbol, a paper form or a poster, a meeting room, a telephone or a membership card, or a digital platform. With technology we form as multitudes (Virno 2004, 84).

The framework of a society isn't only institutional, but also technical: societies have a technical condition. It needs to be guarded and can't be taken for granted. While the distributed recording of the G20 protests helped to clarify the death of Ian Tomlinson, the US Patent 8,254,902 assigned to Apple shows the vulnerability of this new technical crowd. Granted on August 28, 2012, this patent describes a new method of crowd control: to wirelessly disable the camera on the company's iPhones, or to force the phone to enter 'sleep mode' when entering a sensitive area. The patent names movies, but also says: 'Covert police or government operations may require complete "blackout" conditions' – the censorship of the printed press has found its equivalent.

Technology interacts with the social formation of a people. New forms of control emerge, but the crowd has also changed: digital technology produces a mass of different consistency than the one produced by industrial technologies. While traditional mass media deliver identical news to each member of the public, the mass of the digital Leviathan is a patchwork that consists of some users who have clicked on the link of a search result, the 'friends' on Facebook, the followers on Twitter, or the readers of a blog: the internet is a conglomeration of mini-masses. With the French philosophers Deleuze and Guattari, who helpfully point out the difference between masses and packs (1980, 33), we can describe the

DOI: 10.1057/9781137373502

crowd of mass media as of large quantity, aggregated as a whole, and structured in a one-way hierarchy. The digital public, on the other hand, is better conceptualized as an aggregation of dispersed entities, some of which consist of packs of a small and restricted number, some of which don't even form a group but consist of individual voices. All drift off in different directions and are impossible to fix down, as they are in a constant flux of qualitative metamorphosis. This not only gives the crowd a new potential, but it also poses a risk: how does a crowd in constant flux claim their citizen rights of free speech when confronted with new ways of censorship? Offering resistance often presents a problem for the scattered crowd, and it isn't much defended by society either.

When the digital public started to gather in packs; when it used the new platforms to write and publish their own versions of events, or correct news articles; when this public blogged about issues and tweeted its opinions, journalists behaved not very different from the first Leviathan – for quite a long time the government had suspected the press to destabilize society, thus censored it. In the beginning of the digital era, numerous published articles and debates brought to light the same tremendous irritation on the part of the journalists. And to be fair, one could say that the journalists were not the only ones; the rise of the digital public irritated the public as much as the journalists. With journalism being the point of reference of societies' truths, it was no wonder that a lot of reservations came to light: if everybody can publish at nearly zero cost, does this lower the standards? Blogs lack the checks and balances of the public media and have no declared commitment to accuracy. Worse still, it can even be a disadvantage for journalism that it is bound to facts, while on the internet everyone can publish rumours and break the news. Search engines, social media, and blogs were seen as a parasite of journalistic media that take away the jobs of traditional journalists. And isn't digital media forcing the journalistic voice to become louder, simpler, and more stupid?

The opposing side replied to these objections that brash voices as well as the publishing of rumours and copying articles have always been part of journalism. Likewise, journalism has always been split into television, radio, newspapers, magazines, which could be further broken down into tabloid and investigative journalism, news reporting and trade journals, financial news, and women magazines, and so on. In short, fragmentation has always been a feature of the public. However, what causes all these worries in the end is the following: with digitalization, two different

DOI: 10.1057/9781137373502

aspects of the public are drifting apart that before have been closely linked. Hannah Arendt pointed out both of them, when she analysed the concept of 'the public':

> The term 'public' signifies two closely interrelated but not altogether identical phenomena: It means, first, that everything that appears in public can be seen and heard by everybody. ... Second, the term 'public' signifies the world itself, in so far as it is common to all of us. (Arendt 1958, 50 and 52)

While the first meaning of 'public' refers to being *accessible by all* – 'be seen and heard by everybody', the second meaning of 'public' refers to being *relevant for all* – 'common to all of us'. In the era of industrialization, these two aspects have been interwoven: the news on a mass medium were to be seen and heard by everybody, and also tried to be common to all of us (often to the extent that we accused mass media of gross oversimplification of our utterly complex world). In the era of digitalization, however, although what is published on the World Wide Web can potentially be seen and heard by everybody, it isn't necessarily also common to all of us. The public that once had the task to monitor social and political power is now occupied by a babble of voices, and profound observations are next to private nonsense. This rise of irrelevant news easily accessible by everybody is a new phenomenon commonly referred to as 'cat blogging'. Now cats are surely confident enough animals to accept the burden of becoming a blue print for irrelevant news – their success on the internet via lolcats.com or stuffonmycat.com is anyhow out of the question. Implied in the term *cat blogging*, however, is the downturn of a publishing society. The fragmentation of the public poses the threat of a public where everyone can be potentially seen, but where no one is heard. When publishing becomes a private affair and loses public relevance, the individual, instead of being seen, paradoxically disappears under the deluge of individual postings. Arendt writes about this individualization, that:

> men have become entirely private, that is, they have been deprived of seeing and hearing others, of being seen and being heard by them. They are all imprisoned in the subjectivity of their own singular experience, which does not cease to be singular if the same experience is multiplied innumerable times. (Arendt 1958, 57)

Arendt's concern that men have become entirely private is taking on a new dimension in the digital era. Algorithms have created the situation of a new 'private publicness', and while this private publicness can be very useful, it

DOI: 10.1057/9781137373502

shouldn't get confused with the public sphere. A good and very interesting example for this is Kickstarter, a crowd-funding platform for creative projects. Kickstarter helps to gather money by making use of the digital public. For this, the creators of a project choose a deadline and a minimum funding goal, and then promote their project. Kickstarter has opened new ways of funding for creative projects, however, it isn't a people's new Art Council – the founders themselves were always very aware that there is a difference. A society has own and different interests than the sum of its individual people. As a broad popular appeal is essential to get a lot of funders, more complicated and complex projects not easy to access are at a disadvantage. In the case of Kickstarter, using the new private publicness adds an opportunity for cultural projects to get funded, but it doesn't replace the public investment, which is of a different logic. With Arendt, we can insist that the relevance *for a mainstream* (the majority of people) is something different than the relevance for all – a much more complicated thing.

The interesting example of Kickstarter, however, helps us to understand the relevance of today's journalism. Journalism is bound to the public interest, not to the interest of the majority – otherwise a newspaper would only consist of crosswords, cooking recipes, football reports, and Royal babies. This indicates a different focus: while the digital public usually is made up of a sum of individual people, journalism reports in the interests of a society. Its focus can coincide with the digital public – of course, individual people can also pursue the interest of a society – but in general its focus is of a slightly different manner: journalism not only establishes and fosters a common ground of facts, but it also acts as a social interface by which means our societies negotiate what is relevant for all. Finally, news brands deliver their content to a much bigger audience. This is why the BBC warns in its 'Guidelines, Section 7.4.8' to carefully consider the usage of material that was placed in the public domain of the digital public pointing out the impact of the reuse (BBC 2013b). Consequently, one can say that there is a digital public, when something becomes *potentially accessible for everybody*, and there is a journalistic public, when something becomes *potentially accessible* and is *relevant* for all.

The digitalization of the press

Digitalization is challenging journalism in various ways, but challenge is nothing new for journalism. Historically, journalism has not only

DOI: 10.1057/9781137373502

operated at the border of viability but also under the threat of censorship. In our secular societies, it is a job that is bound to truth, therefore never just a job but a vocation. Regardless if one does journalism as an editor, a reporter, a programmer, or a publisher, one never got into journalism because she or he aims to err on the side of caution. Now that algorithms have become the new printing presses, journalism has to face the disruptive force of digitalization. It confronts it with the following three aspects: a broadening of the distribution of journalism that results in a restructuring of its business and affects its production as it becomes a process.

Digitalization has broadened the reach of journalism in a global and a ubiquitous direction. The technical condition of a World Wide Web has widened the scope globally. As British media institutions such as *The Guardian* and *The Daily Mail* have more traffic from the US than from the UK, they reorganized their journalism: they operate as a networked organization, which means a small desk formerly filled by a foreign correspondent has grown to become a news room. But digitalization also had a ubiquitous effect on media. By 2010 the British were spending half their day engaging in media and communication activities, on average 7 hours and 5 minutes of the 15 hours and 45 minutes they are awake, as a survey of 1,138 adults revealed (Ofcom Communications Market Report 2010). An activity that would rise even more. The new omnipresence of media had effects on journalism. Earlier, journalists simply had to consider their target group. Now they also had to take into account in which situation their product would be received. In addition to the old question of who it is a journalist actually addresses, there is a new concern with the type of device through which the journalism is consumed: the technical condition, which is by now truly multimedia: people communicate on a social platform when they watch television; they reach out to their phone and go online when reading the news on a paper; they are using new and old media side by side.

Those two tendencies have massively broadened the reach of journalism. In 1996, shortly before the internet became a mass medium for publishers, *The New York Times* had a weekday circulation of 1.17 million. Fifteen years later in September 2011 the circulation was still 1.15 million copies, only now its journalism reached additional readers through digital distribution. Forty-seven million users read the newspaper monthly online, among them are 324,000 digital subscribers – *The New York Times* had just put up a metered modelled pay wall that quickly would

DOI: 10.1057/9781137373502

be accepted. In Britain, all daily newspapers have suffered a decline of their circulation. In October 2000, *The Guardian* still sold on an average weekday 393,953. In October 2011 it only sold 230,541, but more than 60 million readers visited the site in the same month. Even the circulation of the biggest German magazines, *Der Spiegel*, hasn't changed much yet. In 1989 as well as in 2011 it were both around million, but in 2011 the news brand, German leader in the market of digital news, added with *Spiegel Online* monthly approximately 10 million unique users. Digitalization has broadened the audience for journalism even though in the long run readers might welcome print only as a luxury exception.

In the history of journalism, shifts such as those are nothing new to news organizations. At the turn of the nineteenth century one of the oldest news media, the newspaper, shifts its attention from political wings to target groups as the newspaper trade was in crisis. Among others, *The Times* and its chief competitor *The Standard* faced a sharp decline in finance. It was time for a 'new journalism'. Hundred years before becoming a manifesto for American writers, the brothers Harold and Alfred Harmsworth introduced a new approach to journalism with a change of style and tone to create a 'newspaper for everyone'. The long, complicated, and hard to understand reports were replaced with short articles and bigger headlines for a quick overview – text journalism as we still know it today. While conservative journalists talked about the decline of journalism, readers embraced it: within three years the *Daily Mail* as the prototype of 'New Journalism' acquired half a million readers a day, which grew in the fourth year to 700,000 (Herd 1952, 153, 222 and 242). A mass market emerged, and with it a target audience and a reader model that represented the intended reader. Challenged by technology, 100 years later journalism is again forced to reinvent itself.

The second aspect is the business of journalism, which finds itself intensely struck by the technical gesture of digitalization, fragmentation. This demands of the press a fundamental adaptation of their business model, which can no longer rely on the simple two-armed revenue stream of advertising and subscription. While both are still important sources of income, they can no longer be taken for granted. Thus, the press as well as the broadcasting services had to open themselves up to a whole new revenue delta. Already in 2009 the UK had become the first Western economy in which advertisers spent more money on the internet than on television. In the US, the internet finally surpassed newspaper ads in 2010 to become second only to television. Mobile internet pushes

DOI: 10.1057/9781137373502

both of these numbers further. The problem for old media is, however, that ad spending is not simply shifting to their new online versions. The bigger part of the digital advertising money is invested in new digital advertising formats with listings next to search, displays on internet portals, social media platforms, directly on campaign websites, or with mobile phone applications. For the launch of its new product Cillit Bang, the company Reckitt Benckiser, for example, restricted its marketing to the platform Facebook. But digital also multiplied their opportunities for payment and advertisement: newly bundled and combined in different ways, their content can now serve different purposes – an opportunity of self-aggregation, which was only slowly discovered. Looking for new sources of revenue, news publishers had also to think about journalism with a new approach: journalistic experts are managing contemporary information, and there is no reason why this information should only be delivered as journalism, and not in other formats. Different forms of what was once called a 'line extension' are being explored. As Alan Rusbridger, the editor of *The Guardian*, explains: 'Once you get beyond the idea of bits of text on a page, there are other ways of telling stories and of engagement with the readers, which include maybe education, or training, or events' (private communication).

The Guardian stages several conferences each year focusing on media, environment, international development aid, or the public service sector. To take this a step further, it also started to open its building to its readers through 'The Open Weekend Festival'. In March 2012, 5,000 readers bought tickets for the two-day event during which journalists questioned politicians, interviewed artists, discussed political topics, explained how to produce a good crossword riddle, and lively debated aspects of contemporary life with their readers. *The New York Times* also has a 'Knowledge Network' (2013). In collaboration with educational institutions it hosts adult education, with some courses given by their journalistic experts directly. Will news organizations one day take their place next to universities?

Finally, digitalization transformed reporting: the omnipresence of digital media has, of course, changed vast parts of the production of journalism and led to a restructuring of first the newsrooms and then of whole organizations. Television and radio, newspapers and magazines use the new digital possibilities to open themselves up to the digital public using different technologies and interfaces such as Twitter, Facebook, data visualizations, comments, or crowd sourcing. Emily Bell, the former

DOI: 10.1057/9781137373502

director digital of *The Guardian*, once described this mindset as not doing journalism on the web, but journalism with the web. One of the first examples that made use of the digital possibilities on a large scale was *The Guardian's* investigation of the parliamentary expenses scandal regarding expenses claims made by members of the UK Parliament. Triggered by a leak and subsequently published by *The Telegraph*, examples of misdemeanours included a Tory MP who claimed £1,645 for a duck house to be put on a floating island in his pond, and a former Labour minister who claimed £16,000 for a mortgage 18 months after the loan had been repaid. However, even for trained journalists the voluminous leaked document with its hundred thousands of pages proved difficult to review. Using the motto 'Investigate your MP's expenses', *The Guardian* uploaded 458,832 pages-long facsimile to their webpage and asked the public to help.

This form of journalism is surely new only in parts; the scoops of investigative journalism has always depended on tips and hints, and a colourful report always made use of eye witnesses – a quality that was pushed further by CNN. Since 2006 the television channel has sought to reach out and integrate its audience further into the news. They first started, albeit tentatively, to blog online about other blogs, but took the integration of online content radically to the next step with their mobile phone application that was developed under the guidance of general manager of CNN digital, Kenneth 'KC' Estenson. Launched in 2009, the CNN app placed the users' iReport in a prominent fixed place in the app's dock thereby encouraging the user to film and to actively take part in the news. The outcome of this could already be seen in the coverage of the 2010 Haiti earth quake, where CNN managed to report from places which no reporter managed to reach. Users were also asked to leave email addresses and a phone number so that reporters could contact them as sources, thus enhancing the news channel's reporting.

The New York Times decided for a different approach. Instead of crowd sourcing news coverage, it analysed material that its journalist Robert Mackey, who at that time was the head behind its breaking news blog 'The Lede', had found on video platforms or elsewhere on the web. The Lede was used for a transparent analysis of these findings as well as for background analyses. *The New York Times* preferred not to use crowd sourcing for fact gathering, but approached the crowd for opinion gathering. Its multimedia experts Jon Huang and Aron Pilhofer created software and developed database tools in which the readers' answers would be still readable, while being part of a larger visual story. The model they came

DOI: 10.1057/9781137373502

up with was similar to the 'Opinion State' of the State Department. After Bin Laden was killed in May 2012, 13,864 readers answered, for example, the questions: 'Was his death significant in our war against terror? And do you have a negative or positive view of this event?'

Of course, public broadcasters are also approaching the digital public. The BBC actively uses social media platforms to engage with their audience for news and other programs. Robin Morley, the social media lead for BBC English Regions, made this explicitly clear to his colleagues in 2012 when he wrote: 'All English Regions journalists and programme-makers to have/develop a working knowledge of social media tools and their editorial value' (Morley 2012). While journalists have added digital tools to their reporting with due diligence, much has changed. Alan Rusbrigder is convinced for the better of journalism: 'As journalists it is our aim to get to the truth. Generally trying to capture other narratives or voices, is going to produce something that is more likely to get to the truth. So we ought to welcome these new techniques' (private communication). Accommodating forms of response that make truth 'a much more plastic concept' as he puts it, also adds a new term to the journalistic ethics: 'transparency'. In today's media organizations, Simondon's term of a 'technical reality' is within our grasps.

In the history of our democratic societies, journalism has controlled power that is voted into the office. Today, society isn't formed just by politics, but also by technology. Shouldn't journalists therefore engage with technology as much with politics? From tuning net neutrality and the internet protocol, to the platforms that represent a place to shape public opinion, to our not so private data uploaded to the cloud, all of these places are technical realities that shape our social interaction. In effect, the internet didn't result in the surrender of the journalistic ethic. On the contrary, it broadened its scope.

It is interesting to note that similar to journalism, in which private companies represent public interests, new media companies have likewise adopted ethical principles. When Google stopped censoring their search results in China in 2010, the media reporter of *The New York Times*, David Carr, stated rightly that the company 'held itself to a higher standard', and wrote: 'Running a media company requires a set of values that selling a can of soda or a pair of sneakers doesn't' (2010). Following a higher standard, however, the digital public took its place at the side of the journalistic public – never before has mediated information been that ubiquitous in everyday life. In today's media landscape they add an

DOI: 10.1057/9781137373502

important third voice to the following dilemma: while media moguls such as Rupert Murdoch and others are eager to expand their media empires and try to avoid regulations, the politicians deciding over these regulations are interested in getting a good press. Therefore politicians and press people are both regarded by the other with favour, and in journalism this can be called a serious conflict of interests. Democracy might have emerged from pieces of broken pottery to more sophisticated forms of communication, but to balance politics and to speak the truth is no less vulnerable than it was back in Socrates' times in Athens. How can today's media democracy ensure the distance between politics and the press? And what is this new digital public out there, powered by algorithms instead of printing presses or broadcasting licenses? Can we direct a viral logic?

DOI: 10.1057/9781137373502

5
The Digital Public

Abstract: *This chapter contributes to sociology of media by developing criteria exemplary for the digital public. Discussing social media, blogs, and viral videos, the chapter develops categories to describe the internet as a 'potential mass medium' that gathers masses spread territorially as well as in time. Referring to the use of Twitter for example in Egypt's Arab Spring, the chapter also finds new rules of digital mass reporting: here, a plurality of immediate voices enabled to evaluate an event by constructing the sameness in different perspectives. This also means that digital media imposes on the public an active usage of its reasoning, which triggers an interesting change of the traditional negative reception of the masses.*

Keywords: 'digital public', 'public sphere', 'Transformation of the Public Sphere', 'digital journalism', 'viral communication', Twitter, data journalism

Mercedes Bunz. *The Silent Revolution: How Digitalization Transforms Knowledge, Work, Journalism and Politics Without Making Too Much Noise.* Basingstoke: Palgrave Macmillan, 2014. DOI: 10.1057/9781137373502.

DOI: 10.1057/9781137373502

The internet, as the backbone of the digital public, initiates a replay of the process newspaper readers experienced in the nineteenth century: they are assembled as crowds that physically do not have to gather. However, digitalization doesn't lose its disruptive force, once it reached out for the masses. As we will see in this chapter, the new technology assembles them in a different way, profoundly changing the qualities of a crowd.

During the industrial era, crowds were mostly perceived as a mob. They were feared equally for violence, conformist behaviour, and homogeneous tendencies. This problematic reception of the masses starts with the descriptions of the Scottish journalist Charles Mackay (1841), who published one of the first books on the madness of crowds. Among other things, he discerned a facile nature when it comes to economic bubbles, Middle East crusades, and silly shapes of beards. When the French Sociologist Gustave Le Bon further introduced the topic with his book *The Crowd: A Study of the Popular Mind* (1894), he added that they were easy to manipulate. An observation his influential colleague Sigmund Freud agreed upon. In *Mass Psychology* (1921) he denoted that the intellectual capacity of a group is always below that of an individual. In Germany, the critical thinking of the Frankfurt School finally crushed the reputation of the masses. In their book *Dialectic of Enlightenment* (1944, 94) Adorno and Horkheimer described them as a group of alienated individuals steered by the suggestions of a cultural industry and manipulated accordingly by the logic of capitalism. In a nutshell, the masses of an industrial society are something to be worried about. Now digitalization delivers some new potential. A new social force unfolds, which could fundamentally change our perception of crowds.

Since the internet covers our world with information, and digital gadgets accompany us everywhere, crowds have changed. To a certain extent, this isn't a headless crowd on a leash anymore: now they can update their knowledge any time or report their experience in or even as a crowd, to throw light at the events around them while they happen. The so-called flash mob – a term coined in 2003 to describe a loose group of people that assemble suddenly in a place to perform a certain act – has proven that people can collaborate in a new way. Additionally, collectively gathered knowledge has been acknowledged as quite useful, and projects such as the free online encyclopaedia Wikipedia have earned some academic respect. Very soon the new qualities of the masses drew some attention. Books researching the new phenomenon started to focus on *The Wisdom of Crowds* (Surowiecki 2004) and found some *Cognitive Surplus* (Shirky 2011);

DOI: 10.1057/9781137373502

they described them as new virtual communities (Rheingold 2002) and conceded that 'change happens when people come together' (Shirky 2008). Instead of being defined by their deficits, the crowds that emerge in the era of digitalization are obviously of a different quality: they share knowledge, and are able to perform an act of self-control.

This new phenomenon is more interesting, as the topics of maddening are still the same: comparing Mackay's time with the beginning of the twenty-first century, we must admit that we still invest in financial bubbles as if the 'tulip mania' had never happened, and while crusades may be a thing of our past, we still participate in acts of war in the Middle East, not to speak of the fact that we fancy silly beards to this day. Nevertheless we now talk about the 'wisdom of crowds'. Consequently, as we humans haven't changed, this can only be the effect of the technology that gathers us together in a new way. In order to identify this new quality, one must compare the digital technology with the distribution technologies of our past.

Technologies that distribute information have always been an important foundation of forming a public: it was the invention of steam trains that first allowed the local newspapers to broaden their readership and finally become supra-regional. In England, after paper boys rode on their bicycles, newspaper trains travelled the country. Similar to nations fighting over territory, news brands started to fight for their expansion. While the British Empire annexed the two formerly independent Boer republics in 1899 and expanded their colonial empire, the London newspapers, led by the *Daily Mail*, decided to enter the Manchester region using a newspaper train; the sales of the Manchester's *Guardian* had dropped due to its critical view on the Boer war, and the London papers aimed to grab a share of the market by transporting their morning papers in time (Herd 1927, 61). This anecdote makes apparent that it needed an immense effort of machines, man, and material to transform geographically scattered crowds into a national public. As a newspaper train was a tremendously expensive and risky investment, this had two effects: First, most efforts were profit driven and journalism reached out for a mass by focusing on the lowest common denominator, which wasn't very critical, of course. Second, the costly distribution guaranteed that smaller players couldn't afford the needed investment to become big, and bigger players only had to fear the competition from other big players. The politics inherent to this distribution were decidedly non-pluralistic.

DOI: 10.1057/9781137373502

Reaching out to the recipients, however, changes fundamentally with the development of a digital public. On the internet, the channels of distribution are neither costly nor complicated. The transfer of data and the calling of its IP-address may be two different technical acts, but due to the internet's high speed they seem to us humans as if they happen in one go. Furthermore, being part of a universal address system technically connects every single person with all other participants. Thus, each open posting on the internet is available to the billions inhabiting the 'global village' (McLuhan 1962). Unless access is denied this means that everything on the internet is always already distributed, and therefore one can categorize the internet as *a potential mass medium*. Technically, this cuts the costs for reaching out to the public a lot, which establishes a media environment of more equality. The *Guardian*'s editor Alan Rusbridger described this transformation as an astonishing discovery for journalists: 'We' – he referred to journalists like himself – 'like creating things – words, pictures, films, graphics – and publishing them. So, it turns out, does everyone else' (2010). Compared against the era of industrialization, digital technology takes away some control of the distribution from big media corporations. Not only big players but everyone, who is connected to the internet and has some media literacy, can speak up in public. For this, the blog *Boing Boing* is a good example.

Mark Frauenfelder and Clara Sinclair founded the project as a 'directory of wonderful things' in 1988. Of course, at that time it still was published in print. The American fanzine reached a humble circulation of maximum 17,500 printed copies. Focusing on technology, weird science, futurism, and left-wing politics, *Boing Boing* became a web-only publication in 1996 to be relaunched in the format of a weblog in 2000. Still holding on to the quirky side of things, it was the change from print to digital publishing that made its readership grow vastly. In 2010 boingboing.net was attracting 2.5 million unique visitors each month as well as blue-chip advertisers such as American Express and Verizon. It is fair to say that it has reached the size and the advertising clients of former mass media, which now find themselves next to odd headlines announcing: 'The unbearable sadness of winter tomatoes', '250 indie games you must play', 'Mean things authors say about each other', or 'ICANN votes to roll out 400–800 top-level domains'.

Boing Boing, for example, demonstrates that the decrease of cost allows formerly marginal and more critical voices to find a broad public. Different to the industrial age, the logistic effort doesn't incentivize

DOI: 10.1057/9781137373502

publishers anymore to lower the standards. With the rise of the internet, more people have access to publishing than ever before. However, this new equality comes with a new problem – in the age of digitalization, the important ideal of 'equality' continues to stay a political issue. In sum, we can say that in the era of industrialization, being 'free' also had to mean an equal chance to use this freedom, but the equalizing effort that comes with ensuring this by regulating sometimes threatened a person's individual freedom. With a medium such as the internet, this individual freedom was granted as there is no journalistic gatekeeper between the people and the public. Now, the access to publishing wasn't elite anymore but equal. But a new threat emerged: with the internet, any opinion can be publicly published but is threatened to vanish unheard-of in the Long Tail of equal niches. At least for a while. For in digitalization, this isn't whole story. What is published might not be immediately received, but could always be discovered later.

The archive of the present

In our non-digital prehistory, we always were able to get a more detailed knowledge about the past than about the present. Historic studies had researched, for example at the time of World War I, the status of mining, car manufacturing, likewise the role of football, the nutrition of children, or the status of communication technology. We were able to find studies on epidemics in Europe or get detailed information about the political situation in India at that time. All this knowledge had been collected and written up and waited in our libraries to be researched if needed. By contrast with our potential knowledge about our past, before the internet we were rather innocent about our present; apart maybe from the American president with his hosts of experts and network of advisers collecting knowledge from all over the world. This should change with the internet. Now everyone could follow the present course of events as we report and comment in blogs and social networks a daily range of personal and professional events. These countless contributions fill the internet as a media archive recording of what is happening at the present time. We had established an archive of the present.

As the historic archive systematically lists documents recording the past, the internet systematically lists present information. The World Wide Web, for example, uses its uniform resource locator (url), to match

DOI: 10.1057/9781137373502

a present document with a unique address. This approach is systematic, but with its overwhelming content it seems as confusing as London's British Library's collection of 14 millions. While being similar to our traditional archives, the content is overwhelming; different from them, the digital information isn't put in shelves. It rests in a contextual cloud of semantic niches held together by algorithms, and this means the digital public relies on its own logic of communication and attention earlier described as 'The Long Tail' (Anderson 2006).

While there is reason to question 'The Long Tail' as a promising economic model (cf. Chapter 3), Anderson states correctly a new phenomenon: if something is packed away in the Long Tail, it doesn't mean it also is once and for all forgotten. On the contrary, in the era of digitalization, algorithms search past contextual clouds to bring once forgotten moments to the horizon of the present. His striking example: *Touching the Void* (1988) written by the British mountain climber Joe Simpson had in his time been a modest success. In effect, it was nearly forgotten. Ten years after it was published, suddenly its sales rose. It became a bestseller. What had happened? A new book with a similar topic, Jon Krakauer's *Into Thin Air* (1997), was nominated for Pulitzer Prize and came to be a publishing success. Krakauer's book also rekindled the attention for *Touching the Void*, which finally even outsold the newer book. Being pushed, among others, by recommendation algorithms of online booksellers, it became a viral hit. On the internet it only looks as if something ended up in the backwater of the medium, but in its niches nothing is ever forgotten – a thrill as much as a threat.

As digital information has the potential to be constantly rediscovered, it is obvious that the internet follows a different logic of media, thereby completing the journalistic public. In comparison, the journalistic logic of attention can be described as event-driven. It is structured by two moments: new events and anniversaries of past events. That issues, which don't fit these categories, have a hard time attracting journalistic attention is well known (Gans 1979). The digital public, on the other hand, is interest-driven, as Alan Rusbridger (2010) pointed out when he replied to the argument that Twitter users have a short attention span: 'They will be ferreting out and aggregating information on the issues that concern them long after the caravan of professional journalists has moved on.' This expands the maximum usability period of information. The joke of the British media tsar Alfred Harmsworth – '*The Times* thinks that news, like wine, improves by keeping' (Kitchin 1925, 84) – by which he mocked

DOI: 10.1057/9781137373502

in 1902 the struggling British newspaper for notoriously announcing events too late has 100 years later become a reality. Now news can
improve their value with storage: interests and not events drive the logic
of the digital public.

This fundamentally changes our everyday behaviour of reaching out
for information. Worried journalists noted that the digital public is no
longer afraid to miss out on something. Often, the public doesn't even
make an effort to actively catch up with the news. 'If the news is that
important, it will find me', was the much-cited remark of a student the
media journalist Brian Stelter (2008) reported on, when he studied for
The New York Times new ways of dealing with political news. After he
observed how young people used findings and recommendations of
friends to make their way through the information overload of the digital age, he rightly claimed that 'finding political news online, the young
pass it on'. That way, the viral logic of the digital public rose, for which
the video 'Did You Know?/Shift Happens' is a good example.

Published online in 2006, watched by millions and an inspiration to a
lot of copy cats, the video compiled statements about globalization and
the information age. It was created by Karl Fisch, director of technology
of a High School in Colorado, when he was asked to speak at the yearly
school faculty meeting in 2006. Pulled together in PowerPoint, the video
presents a range of interesting figures such as: 'China will soon become
the number one English speaking country in the world' or 'Nintendo
invested $140 million in research and development...while the U.S.
federal government spent less than half as much on research and innovation in education.' Fisch uploaded the video on his blog 'Fischbowl',
where it caught some attention in the education scene. Another educa-
tor, the book author David Warlick, blogged about it and initiated a
digital conversation. Over time, more and more bloggers commented
on it. Finally, half a year after it appeared online, two users posted it on
YouTube and added additional video portals to it. Five years later, it had
been watched on YouTube over 5.5 million times with figures still rising,
while the video aggregating site Glumbert.com also recorded 4 million
views. Several subsequent versions had the same success, one of them
commissioned by the British magazine *The Economist* for their Media
Convergence Forum in New York. The video had not only become viral,
it had become a 'meme', a term coined by the British psychologist Susan
Blackmore (2000) for describing different replications of an object or
pattern when spreading from one person to another.

DOI: 10.1057/9781137373502

Viral communication, however, isn't spreading just by chance. While its ways can't be controlled, it can be supported; experts call this 'massaging the stream'. When publishing his video Karl Fisch, for example, follows certain rules that accelerate its viral aspect. These rules can be summed up as the three Cs: 'content', being 'catching', and 'capacity'. Its title 'Did you know?' addressed the viewer directly thereby promising a personal merit. Once started, the video catches the viewer's attention directly when after just a few seconds it proclaims a sexual allusion: 'sometimes size does matter'. And third, its six minutes is even manageable to view in an office situation, thereby not overexerting the users' attention span. In addition to these three rules, the title keeps it simple and describes the video, which makes it easy to be found by search engines and humans alike.

Contrary to traditional media, the focus of viral communication isn't about reaching a huge mass at one go. In the beginning 'Did you know?/ Shift happens' drew attention rather slowly to reach a million views only after half a year: being based on links, being embedded, republished and linked to, its distribution accelerated slowly from one individual to another. Thus we can say, the viral logic of the digital public gathers masses that aren't just spread territorially but also in time, and repetition is its drive. Consequently, it is also important to make viral content accessible in a technical as well as a juridical way: by using the Creative Comments license, Fisch signalized that it was legal to republish it on other platforms and sites; he also allowed remixing it. Additionally, the upload on a video portal such as YouTube enabled a technically easy sharing by embedding the video or copying the link. As in a potential mass medium the distribution is given, the crucial moment of the viral logic is repetition: it is repetition by which a video such as 'Did you know?/ Shift happens' gathers attention and allows the presentation, that once was created for an assembly hall of a school, to reach millions. It doubles its potential to go viral, if something can be repeated and shared, if it can be easily used anew and legally get remixed. Culturally, this imposes an interesting shift: once our arts used the concept of mimesis as a recapitulating repetition of reality, or even as its appropriation, as the study of the historic Erich Auerbach (1953) on the representation of reality has shown. By depicting reality, art appropriated it through creative repetition. Now part of this reality is given as media. Here repetition – passing it on – leads our attention to what should be focused upon. And in a certain way, it also plays its part in acquiring what we consider as 'truthful'.

DOI: 10.1057/9781137373502

Reported by a choir of voices

Whenever information becomes news or a fact, it has been checked or reassessed by experts, journalists, or historians, for example, who speak to witnesses and check sources on being trustworthy. When we evaluate the digital stream of information in the archive of the present, however, we proceed differently: on the internet, one can establish something as potentially factual, when independently from each other different statements all describe the same. In the words of Hannah Arendt, one can say that the truth of the digital public derives its 'significance from the fact that everybody sees and hears from a different position' whereby we experience a 'sameness in utter diversity' (Arendt 1958, 57).

It is interesting that this approach to a fact has been used during the historic event of the Arab Spring, when the only available information had often been postings on platforms such as Twitter. Using this service during the protests for the resignation of Egypt's former leader Mubarak in early 2011, young Egyptians let an international English-speaking audience know what was happening. On February 2, the day after President Hosni Mubarak had given a speech, some of the many tweets from Cairo's Tahrir Square read as follows:

> **Gsquare86** Pro-Mubarak march now coming into Tahrir in 'a big number' and it will get ugly http://yfrog.com/h3zsgekj *13:39:10*
>
> **Sandmonkey** 1000 pro Mubarak demonstration is heading towards Tahrir. The military is withdrawing. This will get ugly quick #jan25 *13:40:24*
>
> **TravellerW** INCREDIBLE standoff between pro-change and pro-Mubarak demos at Tahrir NOW #Egypt #jan25 http://twitpic.com/3vqkcp *13:40:49*

While time stamps of their postings document nearly the same moment – 13:39:10, 13:40:24, and 13:40:49 – independently from each other these Twitter users (among others) describe the same incident. Some of them also link to pictures that visualize the situation: a large group of Mubarak followers is coming towards Tahrir Square where other people demonstrate against the old regime. An hour later the situation had escalated:

> **norashalaby** He couldn't beat us with his state security so he sends baltagiya [gangs of paid thugs] to terrorize us. Down w the dictator #Jan25 *14:41:17*
>
> **3arabawy** Plainclothes thugs (police) are on horses now, trying to storm Tahrir Square, with whips! #Jan25 *15:01:23*
>
> **Sandmonkey** Camels and Horses used by Pro Mubarak protesters to attack Anti-Mubarak protesters. This is becoming literally a circus. #jan25 *15:04:27*

DOI: 10.1057/9781137373502

These personal impressions light up a moment in time when hardly any other information on the course of events is available. Their individual perspectives share a certain 'sameness' in covering the event, and it is this 'sameness' – the repetition of the same incidents – that signifies us what 'truthfully' happens. To a certain extent, their tweets and messages are pushing beyond the instant pictures we know from live reporting. Instead of a reporter who was witnessing an event with professional emotional distance, these people *took part* in the event. They didn't report what was happening to others but to them, and this transforms the readers of their tweets, us, into their witnesses. Thus, their relation to truth is inherently different from the distant reporting of the journalistic public.

Only later when their postings on Twitter alongside that of others were published in the book *Tweets from Tahrir* (Idle and Nunns 2011), these voices had been vetted: Gsquare86 aka Gigi Ibrahim is a socialist activist; Sandmonkey aka Mahmoud Salem runs the most widely read Egyptian blog in English called Ranting of a sandmonkey.org; TravellerW is an economic consultant blogging at travellerwithin.com; norashalaby aka Nora Shalaby is an archaeologist and activist, and 3arabawy aka Hossam el-Hamalawy is a blogger, journalist, and photographer. Their approach towards truth can be described as *genuine* instead of objective, with immediacy as a peculiar quality not ousting but completing a journalistic approach: it is the *immediacy* of the digital communication that allows us recipients to become part of an individual moment, while at the same time the *plurality* of immediate voices enables us to evaluate the event by constructing the *sameness* in these different perspectives. Following the Arab Spring on Twitter, people experienced a personal connection while they were gathering the facts from the stream of tweets and became digital witnesses of a revolution. In sum, we can say that the crowds gathered by the digital public are not only smart because wherever they are, they can reach out to information; they also need to process this information much more actively, in order to establish a 'sameness' in the plurality of perspectives. This far more active approach of gathering the facts is a typical conjuncture of the digital public and also found in data journalism, which often directly links or displays the source material.

When data journalism allows access to the original files, it thereby often transforms the digital public into a witness of a bygone moment. The website Bishop-Accountability.org, a non-profit corporation from Massachusetts launched in 2003, follows this approach. Its task is to

DOI: 10.1057/9781137373502

document sex abuse cases related to the Roman Catholic Church by displaying hundreds of uploaded files on church administration and the abuse crisis. On one document, a facsimile letter, we can see the coat of arms that shows three cross crosslets crowned by a bishop's mitre. Below that is printed 'Diocese of Davenport, Davenport, IOWA'. To fit in with the coat of arms, someone has set the date written by a typewriter neatly centred: 'October 3, 1958'. This letter documents the decision of the Roman Catholic Church to cover up the sexual abuses of one of its priests, James Janssen. The file has obviously been copied several times with a stamp that suggests it has been used in court as 'Exhibit Number 19'. It was written shortly after the sexual correspondence between Janssen and a boy had been discovered by the boy's mother, who had reported the incident to Janssen's bishop, Ralph Hayes. His signature is one of the two we see below the following text:

> I, Maurice J. Dingman, Chancellor of the diocese of Davenport, having before me the Holy Bible which I touch with my hand, having witnessed by my signature the document of suspension – the following words have been underlined – ex informata conscientia, issued by the Most Reverend Ralph L. Hayes, Bishop of Davenport, against Reverend James Janssen, a priest of the said diocese of Davenport, do hereby swear that I will maintain secrecy regarding all facts of the case. (Dingman 1958)

Underneath the text, the type writer had marked two lines for signatures adding their official descriptions: Bishop of Davenport and Chancellor. On the page, their signatures are nearly as big as the body of text. The platform stores additional 66 documents related to Janssen, among these a facsimile of the letter in which the boy confronted the perpetrator with his deed. Sources such as these allow us to gain some insight into what abuse might mean to a human, as reading the letter draws us closer to the case than classical distant reporting.

Quite similar to this approach of Bishop-Accountability.org is Wikileaks, a platform that gained international attention in 2011 after publishing secret documents on the wars in Iraq and Afghanistan. Again, one can find authentic documents that speak for themselves alongside short explanatory evaluations. Launched in 2006, the site run by Editor-in-chief Julian Assange gathers, vets, and publishes source material significant to the public while keeping the identity of their sources anonymous. Coined by the media critic Jay Rosen as 'the first stateless news organization' (2010), it focuses generally on investigative

DOI: 10.1057/9781137373502

material thereby fundamentally transforming the meaning of a 'source': after Wikileaks, the term journalists traditionally used to denote a human witness was likewise applied to files. As the source material gets that comprehensive, it obviously starts to 'speak' for itself. Instead of a human claiming to speak the truth the material claims to be authentic. It isn't just by chance that the file is often published as a digital facsimile or an identical copy of the original digital file, but content and form congruently bear witness of a past moment.

In the digital era, the possibility of gathering material anonymously by using encryption protection became the technical equivalent to the journalistic right to protect confidentiality of sources. Opening these documents allowed the public to gain a deep insight into power games, or the scope of a scandal; Wikileaks had been the first platform that used and specialized in this technology. Soon other platforms will allow the same, some of them run by news organizations or news agencies directly – Wikileaks files of larger volume have already been investigated in collaboration with *The New York Times*, the German *Spiegel* or *The Guardian*, among them the Iraq war logs with about 400,000 documents and the US Department diplomatic cables with 251,287 documents. Not only that small organizations such Wikileaks had a problem getting files of this dimension vetted, more importantly humans couldn't even testify the evidence of the vast files with documents all relating to one another. As Alan Rusbridger wrote about the material *The Guardian* investigated in corporation with Wikileaks: 'There are very few, if any, parallels in the annals of journalism where any news organization has had to deal with such a vast database – we estimate it to have been roughly 300 million words' (2011, 5).

Early data journalism such as the Pentagon Papers *The New York Times* published in 1971 had a volume of 2.5 million words. If we do the math, we can conclude: if one reads ten hour a day crunching 400 words a minute, the reading matter can be finished with after ten days. The 300-million word file Rusbridger is referring to would take a bit longer: 1,250 days of reading or nearly three and a half years. Consequently we can say that a single human, who reads the source material, will have a hard time to get to the truth; soon we even might be confronted with a truth that can't be read anymore by humans. Here the digital brought relief: similar to the invention of the telescope, that allowed seeing stars not visible to the human eye, search engines help to browse the digital information that otherwise isn't accessible.

DOI: 10.1057/9781137373502

Summing up a conclusion, we put forth the following findings:

1   For the objective reporting of an event, journalism isn't the only guardian of our social truths anymore but finds at its side the digital public with its choir of voices.

2   As the witnessing of the digital public happens instantaneously and thus without any chance of vetting, the course of events needs to be extracted from the sameness found in the plurality of voices.

3   Consequently, as one statement could be false, a plurality of independent voices is needed to stabilize the truthfulness of digital content.

Hereby, digital media imposes on the public an active usage of its reasoning: in addition to processing individual perspectives into a more truthful synthesis of an event, the digital public also has to filter potentially false statements. Therefore, the crowds that inhabit the digital public are of a different quality than the masses that haunted the industrial era – it is more than simply an 'audience'. The digital mobs are not only called 'smart' because one can text them on their phones and update their level of knowledge whenever needed. They are called smart, because each individual needs to actively form his or her own view of what is going on. Focusing on this social force of digitalization, it can be said that we are entering a second phase of enlightenment and emancipation: after the autonomous subject, whole crowds are asked to form themselves under the banner of enlightenment: *Sapere aude!* ('Dare to know!')

But are freedom, equality, and fraternity relevant in the internet, or is cash king? Can algorithms assist us with organizing a different world, or are they just forcing us to get organized differently? And if five-minute activism is able to make a difference, can we from now on also make a revolution step by step instead of at one go?

DOI: 10.1057/9781137373502

6
The Silent Revolution

Abstract: *This chapter contributes to political theory by evaluating the participatory potential of digitalization: organizing the world differently. In order to do this, it first looks at the effect of digital media on publicness and new forms of political participation by analysing crowdsourcing platforms such as Ushahidi or Sukey, political campaigns such as Obama's 2008 election campaign, and government schemes such as Open Data. Evaluating those critically, it finds: in the digital era, the reflective audience of Habermas's public sphere is replaced by a more active but also more fragmented audience. Then the chapter shifts its focus from the public sphere to new technologies of distribution which are currently rising with the 'internet of things'. Subsequent to the assessment of this technology by humanities scholars such as Katherine Hayles, Nigel Thrift, or Jordan Crandall, the chapter discusses the critical potential of this internet of things.*

Keywords: organization, 'internet of things', 'Transformation of the Public Sphere', 'crowdsourcing', open data, revolution

Mercedes Bunz. *The Silent Revolution: How Digitalization Transforms Knowledge, Work, Journalism and Politics Without Making Too Much Noise.* Basingstoke: Palgrave Macmillan, 2014. DOI: 10.1057/9781137373502.

'An idea. A single idea from a human mind can build cities', explains Leonardo di Caprio in the film 'Inception' to his actress colleague Ellen Page, while the streets of Paris are bending imaginary in front of their eyes. Di Caprio's phrase resonates communism as an idea. Different than the fictive manipulation of Parisian streets, this was an idea that has actually left traces in a range of our cities – Moscow, Brasilia, or East-Germany's Halle-Neustadt to name but a few. However, the idea di Caprio refers to in Christopher Nolan's noir science-fiction movie is quite different: it isn't anymore focused on crowds taking over state power in order to erect a better world. With the help of dreams, di Caprio's crew plans to smuggle an idea into an executive's subconscious. In the digital era, storytelling finds it more comprehensible for ideas to be placed in a single executive in order to enlighten a corporate dream. The course of events will change, when di Caprio's character is able to enter the sub-conscious of the company's director. In this film of our time, change is driven by business interest. And this means, the role of crowds to change the course of history becomes an idea of our past, the industrial age. In Sergei Eisenstein's 1925 movie 'The Battleship Potemkin', for example, the crowd was still the driving force: in 'The Odessa Steps' sequence of the film, the civilian crowds run down the stairs of Odessa's harbour to be shot by the Tsar's soldiers. They die in solidarity for the idea of justice with the sailors. About 100 years later, this isn't the case anymore. Instead of masses which are solidly united by an idea, it now seems more real to filmmakers that executives are guided by a vision. The utopian threat of the James Bond movies from the 1960s and 1970s – that not the people but futuristic egomaniacs such as Dr. No, Goldfinger, or Stromberg decide the course of history – became ordinary.

These stories that we tell ourselves can be read as symptomatic: the economy has invaded our social dreams and replaced politics, a reversal of roles that isn't much of a surprise. Already in 2005, David Harvey pointed out in his *Brief History of Neoliberalism* that the political idea of democracy has been set aside by a shallow version of economy. To put it simply: in the eighteenth century, when economics became a discipline, Adam Smith explicitly turned away from mercantilism and pleaded that politics be kept off the markets, instead of regulating them or bailing out its banks. For Marx, on the other hand, the economy was fundamentally political, so politics should dictate the rules of the market. At the beginning of the twenty-first century, we live neither in Smith's nor Marx's vision, on the contrary: in terms of import and export of goods and workers we regulate

DOI: 10.1057/9781137373502

markets, while economic players such as our financial services influence politics. That there obviously isn't anymore real balance of powers has led the British journalist John Lanchester to state the 'financial system in its current condition poses an existential threat to Western democracy far exceeding any terrorist threat' (Lanchester 2012; see also Kjaer, Teubner, and Febbrajo 2011). Unfortunately, the traditionally rich debate of this complex and interesting topic – our economy – which can be interpreted in many ways has disappeared. When the stock market boom attracted small shareholders, for example, it wasn't debated as adding capital to the financial system. Instead it was introduced to the public discourse as change: now the financial market isn't a place for the elite anymore, but is turned into a democratic market for everyone. Only that on this market chances are not equal: some people are freer than others, because they have more money to buy shares. In *Democracy and other Neoliberal Fantasies* (2009) Jodie Dean has shown how the political idea of equality became the image campaign of several IPOs justifying further privatization. While here it becomes apparent that democracy has been annexed by a dull version of market economy, its political idea can't be appropriate – the idea of equality can't be bought. Both spheres follow a different logic: the structure of the political sphere is fundamentally different to the economic sphere. Following Hannah Arendt, one can say that the aim of politics isn't to make profit, but to organize the collective living of human beings for the better (whatever that may be): 'it has its end in the postpolitical, highest possibility of human destiny' (Arendt 2005, 83). Economy, on the other hand, manages the important distribution of goods, services, and money with the aim to make profit. Both spheres overlap, but function according to different ideas. The consumer has a choice, but buying isn't the same as voting. It is relevant to understand that democracy isn't built on maximizing self-interest, for self-interest isn't a political idea. It is a poor man's ethos.

This is what 'Inception' makes apparent: a tectonic shift has now become conspicuously normal, while earlier the two spheres had to be arduously worked out – Foucault explained the rise of the 'homo oeconomicus' in a whole lecture in *The Birth of Biopolitics* (Foucault 2008, 282). Thus we can say, in the past, the capacity to act was with the crowds, and people together performed a political act. In the present, change is launched by the economy, which has become the most important player in the conscious of our societies. Consequently, it is of no wonder that at the beginning of the twenty-first century we experienced an 'economization

DOI: 10.1057/9781137373502

of everything'. Eva Illouz (2007) has pointed out how economies' driving force, the profit that is assured by the increase of efficiency and rationalization, has left its old place 'work' to make itself at home in all spheres of life: apart from ruling our markets, it is now also applied to issues of life including education or politics, health, even motherhood, aging as well as friendship, or love. All those spheres, notices Illouz, are transformed according to the logic of efficiency. With this analysis, one could even go further and say: it has become difficult to oppose any alternatives to this, at least anything that isn't simply counterposing, but follows its own and different logic. Religion and politics, science and culture seem to be either old fashioned or already governed by the idea of efficiency. The logic of an economy, that paradoxically always proclaimed competition, triumphs. Its reign is absolute. From here rises an interesting question, which brings us back to Simondon's idea of 'technical ensembles'. If we can assume with Simondon that technology is *disparate* and has its own logic, as discussed in Chapter 3, can digital technology be of valuable assistance? With this question in mind, it is interesting to look into Simondon's idea of a 'technical ensemble' again.

In Simondon's philosophy of technology, a 'technical ensemble' is defined as follows: a 'technical ensemble is itself made up of a number of technical individuals that are arranged in terms of the result of their functioning' (1958, 66). However, this isn't necessarily an arrangement of just technical individuals or machines, on the contrary. For Simondon, human individuals are a natural part of technical ensemble, too: 'The human can be coupled with the machine as equal to equal, as a being that participates in its regulation' (119–120). Of course, Simondon wrote his book *On the Mode of Existence of Technical Objects* (1980) when machines had not been digitalized yet. As machines couldn't exchange communication, the role of the human is put forward as one of a regulator. In this way, man is part of a technical ensemble in an equal communication: he enables the machines to communicate, and by doing so adds a human structure to their way. That technology has developed further to communicate directly, however, doesn't make the human redundant. Following Simondon, the relationship can instead be taken even further. 'The human comprehends machines; he has a role to play between machines rather than over and above them, if there is to be a true technical ensemble' (1958, 138). Here, we should pause for a moment to notice that the 'true technical ensemble' – a remarkable wording, also noticed by Thomas LaMarre (2013, 82) – is the ensemble accompanied

DOI: 10.1057/9781137373502

by man. It becomes obvious that man adds another quality to the technical ensemble, which thereby becomes 'true' ('véritable'). As the ensemble hasn't been incorrect before, 'true' here obviously takes on the meaning of 'more genuine'.

That it becomes true by the interference of man is conditioned by the 'technical reality' as Simondon describes it in another small text about 'Technical Mentality' (2012). Here, he points out that the technical reality is characterized by 'the opening: technical reality lends itself remarkably well to being continued, completed, perfected, extended' (13). Drawn by this train of thought, we find the following questions: How can we extend the technical reality of today, and thereby extend it in a direction somewhere different than the awful one we are currently heading to? After all, a society consists in its organization, and more than ever before the organization of this collective is based on the use of technology. If this is the case – if technology gives an external appearance to what is collective, as Virno (2006) has said following Simondon – then we experience the emergence of an interesting question: can we use technology to build a more just society than the existing? If society and technology are linked and can be addressed as an ensemble, can technology help in reorganizing our societies? For in this case, algorithms might be of more value than just efficiently organizing our world economically. A utopian thought, we will come back to in the end, after having looked at some issues of a political approach towards algorithms.

For it is true: at first sight it doesn't look like digitalization offers a lot of help. As we have seen in the previous chapter, it might well push the participation of crowds, but this participation introduces new political problems such as the fact that most of the important online platforms are private enterprises. This comes as no surprise. For a very long time Western governments' approach towards digital technology was very business orientated. In the 1990s, the internet was rarely discussed as a tool that offers new potential to education or our civil society by enabling more participation. Instead, it was referred to as a 'new economy'. Therefore it is of no wonder that at the beginning of the twenty-first century, vast parts of the digital public are built with private means. Like Google, Facebook, Twitter, or Apple's iTunes store, most of the large digital platforms are businesses. As the digital public is built on private platforms, it is situated in a problematic relationship of dependence. This, however, is nothing new: in most Western countries apart from the US, the journalistic public is likewise erected

DOI: 10.1057/9781137373502

on public and privately owned organizations, and private companies find themselves in competition with publicly funded organizations. When we analyse the digital public precisely, we find a similar balance of interests: the weight of millions of users counter the interests of private companies. Contrary to their name, they don't simply *use* the digital public and are its consumers. That is, they actively *participate* in it and thereby form it.

Every day millions of volunteers edit, program, or publish their knowledge in blog postings, or forums, or on Wikipedia, thereby claiming the internet partly as society's commons. Tiziana Terranova (2004) has demonstrated with her excellent book the important role of 'free labour' online. As problematic as this is, it is these users who keep the internet from becoming nothing but another marketplace. On their side, they find software coders, hackers, and technical engineers who look after Open Source projects such as the blogger software 'Word Press', the web server 'Apache', or the web browser 'Firefox' – in fact, one could discuss whether Open Source and Open Access projects should be seen as the public projects of the digital age. Surely, by maintaining and improving the service, they prevent areas from being managed in terms of profit. Thus, we owe it to the users, the volunteers, and the coders that the internet hasn't become another mall, whose only message is the logic of sale. However, we need to acknowledge that compared to traditional media this balance works in a different way.

The traditional counterbalance of the journalistic public is based on its relation to a public sphere. It is not only framed by law, in most countries private journalism also faces competition from public journalism, wherefore the relation of public and private can be described as a 'horizontal balance'. The counterbalance weight of the digital public, on the other hand, has to be understood as vertical: for sure the crowds that inhabit digital media aren't organized in a structure that can compete on a par with private platforms, such as public broadcasting, but the platforms depend on their users' trust. Afraid of losing it, some of them already have received a painful lesson in certain ethical rules; Facebook, for example, enabled the user more and more to control and delete his or her content. Google, on the other hand, always marks advertising by highlighting it visually as sponsoring. These examples show how enterprises are driven by their users to internalize ethical standards. Some of those are actually adopted from traditional media, and just like with traditional media they need to be monitored.

DOI: 10.1057/9781137373502

Interestingly, we likewise find new developments and formats in the sphere of traditional media, regarding the essential separation of editorial content and advertising, for example. Since digital publishing has transformed the actual printing of a magazine into an affordable option, we experience a rise of professional journals that publish something one could call 'journalism': articles of high quality, precisely researched and well written. As they can't claim to be an independent voice, they handle their position transparently and openly list their company in a disclosure. Here transparency, as the disclosure of those rules by which the articles are published, move close to the ideal of an independence (which can never be fully replaced).

Digital companies follow this transparent approach, albeit in different ways. Google pushes the precept that the beliefs and preferences of those who work there shouldn't have an impact on its search results. To give an example: when the search results for 'Jew' delivered an anti-Jewish site at the top of the search results, Google decided to apologize and explain, but not manually alter their results. Instead its search engine, whose co-founder Sergei Brin is of Russian-Jewish origin himself, displays since April 2004 an explanation above the results. In the explanation Google claimed to view the comprehensiveness of its results as an extremely important priority; one can say it pursues the ethical ideal of an algorithmic objectivity. Apple decided to take another path. The company, which also produces smartphones, announced that it is censoring the applications it publishes in its app store one by one. Its guidelines states among other things that it isn't allowed to criticize religion, describe sex, or display the violent abuse of children in apps. This let Apple in late 2011 to remove the game application 'Phone Story' of the Italian company Molleindustria, which was produced to shed some light on 'the dark side of smart phone manufacturing'. The company had tried to raise a discussion of child labour by using a 'serious mini-game'. Examples such as these might make us frown, but they also make something interesting apparent: despite each ethical self-regulation being different, they all aim to withstand the collision with business interests. Similar to journalistic media, digital media companies establish ethics.

Having said that, it needs to be noticed that even ten years after the internet has become a medium for the masses, the protection of their privacy is poor. Companies haven't agreed to allow users comprehensive access to their own individual data. They keep the statistical data they have collected of their users for their own use, and politicians likewise

DOI: 10.1057/9781137373502

have left their citizens in the lurch. Unfortunately, in this case the political sphere also can't replace the critical potential of the digital crowds. For not very different from their counterpart on the streets, the virtual crowds organize their interests mostly in reaction to a cause and event: when Facebook changed its design in October 2010, for example, and confused the private homepage of millions with irrelevant news, hundreds of thousands found themselves online united in groups. In a shock they suddenly realized that Facebook is able to fiddle with their personal content as it pleases. After the platform had a mass of angry users and negative press, they learned from their mistake and promised to apply future changes in closer coordination with their users. The virtual crowds' revolt had forced the company to act more transparently. While voting on 'Terms of Use' and 'Statement of Rights and Responsibilities' shouldn't disguise the fact that Facebook is a private company and not a transparent body such as the BBC, it surely helps to establish a more democratic company culture.

The private condition of the digital landscape is one issue, another one is its virtuality. Rightly the media critic Evgeny Morozov (2011) describes the internet in his book *The Net Delusion* as a double-edged sword that not only allows opponents of a regime to protest, but also the regime to better track opponents. Additionally, protest often isn't much more than a toothless tiger that leaves protesters with the impression of taking part, when in reality it has little or no effect. To click the 'I like' button on a Facebook page devoted to protest or a social cause, to forward an email with a petition or link to it from a blog, or to re-tweet a posting on Twitter – the viral campaign of Kony (2012) is a good example – are all empty gestures. Here taking part in the digital public is nothing but a simulation of a political activity equally problematic as voting without an option for real change. In order to have a political impact, the so-called clicktivism needs to do more than massage the conscience of Western elite. It needs to make a difference. Having said that, it is also a fact that several revolts in the Middle East spread with the help of digital platforms; for example, as discussed in the previous chapter, the Egyptian Revolution that started on January 25, 2011. Here political outrage and the will to refuse corrupt governance were translated into mass protests at Cairo's Tahrir square with the help of digital platforms. Among those was the Facebook group 'We are all Khaled Said', named after a young Egypt's unexplained death in police custody and founded to give the outrage a voice – the internet has started to reshape the organization of social movements (Lovink 2012, 158).

DOI: 10.1057/9781137373502

In effect, there is a particular new political potential in the digital public: in our industrial past, ideas needed to be spread through speeches, books, and newspapers. Back then one read and debated visions in cafés, where opinions were shared until it was time not to interpret the world differently but to change it. The coffee or tea was left behind, as the people got out on the streets with the hope of becoming part of a new and better political truth. Today this basically remains the same, only that these ideas have now found an additional place on social networks: online, we organize ourselves in forums or on fan pages or simply around a '#' on Twitter, and often we don't know each other but share an idea or interest. Here technology can assist, but can't replace the political idea. If political interest is absent, the internet would simply be inhabited by funny cats. When the digital public is inspired with a political idea, however, the toothless tiger shows its claws. In effect, the Egyptian revolution that started on #Jan25 with the help of Facebook and Twitter can be seen as the contemporary version of Emile Zola's letter published on the January 13, 1898 in *L'Aurore* 'J'accuse…!', which has become a generic expression of accusation of the powerful. Consequently, the revolutionary new element of digital platforms isn't the fact that in order to find each other, we now *don't even have to leave the house* anymore. The point is that digitalization makes it much easier to *coordinate ourselves* and *leave the house all at once*. The virtuality of the internet doesn't prevent us from finding each other in reality. Furthermore, digital organization greatly depends on trust: in the beginning of the Occupy protest in 2011, the vast majority of participants followed the call to join the protest without knowing whose call it was exactly. The protest spread from New York's Zuccotti Park into most Western cities. From Twitter to the viral logic of 'Did you know?/Shift happens', from Wikileaks and Boing Boing to Facebook events, the digital public organizes and passes on knowledge, and part of this knowledge is what actually happens out there in the world. As the internet coats our world and technology has become our second nature, the digital public is already testing a technical ensemble. At the moment, it is mainly busy with denoting things, humans, and events in real time. And this has already a political impact. On demonstrations in London, for example.

On digital politics and crowds

When in late 2010, tens of thousands of protesters marched in London against public sector cuts, several hundreds found themselves 'kettled' by

DOI: 10.1057/9781137373502

the British police, that is, they were prevented from leaving a certain area for several hours and couldn't access basic amenities such as water, food, or toilets. To avoid this painful experience in the future, a team of politicized students developed an application called Sukey in 2010. Sukey's aim was simple: the digital service was built to keep people informed about what is going on around them during a demonstration – 'Polly put the kettle on, Sukey take it off again', as the children's song rhymes. In order to allow protesters to sidestep the kettle, a team gathered information about what was happening on the ground by analysing the tweets, texts, and GPS positions of several individual protesters during a demonstration. The Sukey team then updated an online live-map of the protest, and tweeted and texted the news to their subscribers. When the next protest against public cuts was staged in London the following March, thousands accessed the service of Sukey. Kettling was largely avoided. Being informed about an event as it happens influences the formation of the crowd. It becomes a 'smart mob', as the media expert Howard Rheingold (2002) put it. He coined the term impressed by young Japanese who constantly coordinated themselves using their mobile phones. With digital tools, this trend spreads. Using their gadgets, the crowd is also collecting data thereby influencing its own organization, and this usage opens up a whole new range of possibilities.

The project Ushahidi (2013), for example, is set up similar to Sukey, only that it agitates on a much larger scale. In Swahili 'Ushahidi' means 'testimony', or 'witness', and with this aim the Open Source project was launched in Kenya in 2007 – originally it was developed to map numerous reports of post-election violence in the country. As explained in the paper 'Harnessing the crowdsourcing power of social media for disaster relief' (Gao, Barbier, and Goolsby 2011), this approach is centred around a map on which information from SMS, email, Twitter, and the web could be easily visualized to document crisis or human rights abuses that would otherwise be completely undocumented, as journalists or voting monitors can't be everywhere. Soon this was adapted for distinct purposes, among them snow storms in Washington, forest fires in Russia, or power failures in India. Likewise it became a platform to note positive developments: when in Liberia the constitutional referendum took place on August 23, 2011, the map was used to visualize the democratic progress. The participants covered civic voter education activities, media coverage of the election, and other positive events. As the referendum was a test for the upcoming presidential elections, Ushahidi-Liberia (2013) and its

DOI: 10.1057/9781137373502

partner organizations were able to learn about progress or could already note where potentially violence would be likely to erupt and towards whom. During the referendum and the following week, Ushahidi-Liberia received 239 verified messages from trusted participants, who had been trained to use the platform. As in this case, Ushahidi often works in close cooperation with locals who also ensure the correctness of information, for much like cultivating a garden a crowd needs to be maintained. As a platform doesn't automatically form a crowd, most of the Ushahidi projects start with an educational process and a network of locals – they put so to say 'crowdseeding' before 'crowdsourcing'.

Especially with highly sensible events such as elections or catastrophes, crowdsourcing relies on the assistance of people on the ground and needs to go beyond the virtual approach. When the Sudan VoteMonitor team used Ushahidi to monitor the first election in 26 years, for example, they could successfully deal with the problem of false information and dirty data by verifying reports with the help of local action groups. As information must be vetted, over the years the professional team of Ushahidi has developed diverse approaches to match the situations more precisely: apart from the Ushahidi platform, the simplified version 'Crowdmap' was built, as well as a tool named SwiftRiver (2013) to filter and make sense of the massive volume of real-time crisis data. The demand for such an algorithmic sorting tool became apparent in 2010, when after the devastating earthquake in Haiti 25,000 crowdsourced reports came in per day. Despite help, the team couldn't review every single message and thought of ways to use algorithms to maximize precious time.

Digital tools, however, allow more than just mapping events in real time. As tools simplify and assist with communication, the coordination and organization of a crowd fundamentally changes. Levenhus's (2010) case study of Obama's campaign management clearly shows that digital communication enables the crowd to play a much more active part. Kenski, Hardy, and Jamieson (2010) agree in their book that the innovative use of media shaped the 2008 election. Indeed, Barack Obama's first presidential campaign has set benchmarks. Its digital arm was run by the agency Blue State Digital. With 13.5 million digital addresses they didn't just acquire an immense email list the size of prime time television ratings, but they also set free the political and financial potential of an interested crowd and activated millions of people. For this, the mandate of the political campaign – the idea of establishing a personal connection – was taken very seriously: if someone signed up on the website and

DOI: 10.1057/9781137373502

offered to volunteer, the team had made it its duty that within three days the person got a phone call or an email from the campaign staff in order to figure out direct ways of participation. This could result in spreading the word by email or telephone, in hosting private house matinees and debate watching parties, or even in setting up their own activism centre – in total the official campaign was supported by 250,000 individual events. While the so-called 5-minute-activism is often joked about as 'activism light', the labour force of one million people that all donate five minutes of their time can deliver convincing effects. The emphasis on establishing a direct personal connection, that was often coordinated with the help of digital tools, changed the notion of passive supporters to active participation. Digital communication, however, had not only helped to shift the architecture of the campaign organization from some-to-many to many-to-many and made the inclusion and participation of millions possible. It also helped to democratize the campaigns' financial support and brought back plurality.

Before this campaign, the financial support of US presidents showed an economic divide for both parties, Democrats as well as Republicans: in general, 80% of the campaign donations were given in large sums that came from 1% of the population, and this made sure the president would lend his ear to the rich. Reaching out to the people online diminishes this dependence. As the Federal Election Commission (2013) records, in Obama's campaign $335 million were given as micro-donations under $200, a somewhat larger sum than the $112 million in large donations above $2,000. Over the course of Obama's first campaign, the team raised online more than $500 million, according to the director of Obama's new media department, Joe Rospars (Vargas 2008). Even after donors' giving was added to cumulative amounts by a study of The Campaign Finance Institute (Malbin 2009, also Luo 2008), large donors (who gave $1,000 or more in aggregate to Obama) still accounted for a smaller proportion of the total campaign money haul than others – in total the campaign raised $750 million. The change of the financial setting when running for president can have a political effect: money ensures political participation without participating. As technology had eased the financial participation for many, it made Obama a president whose first campaign was financed across classes.

Assisted by digital platforms, citizens can take part in politics more actively, and not only in the campaigning, but also in governance. More and more democratic states have already opened up and added

DOI: 10.1057/9781137373502

participatory elements to their representational mechanisms, the publishing of data, for example. For a government, statistical data is one of the most important instruments to make decisions and shape their population (Foucault 2007, 262), while it also produces statistical data itself from the allocation of its budget to its number of civil servants. Sharing this data makes governments more transparent as it enables the public to scrutinize, for example, government expenses in more detail. But it also allows the citizen to make use of the data themselves. With this, the 'art of government' called statistics (Foucault 2007) opens up to everyone. This provides new economic opportunities as much as it increases potential for political participation, but it also causes a dilemma.

The UK was among the first countries that emphatically took the plunge to share their statistical data for further usage in a machine-readable form. In 2009 the website data.gov.uk was launched, just a few months after its US counterpart which it would soon outnumber in data sets. Sir Tim Berners-Lee and the computer science Professor Nigel Shadbolt have been among the key figures in this successful initiative with thousands of registered developers. The use of the data sets had been quite diverse: the 'Roadworks Database' is, for example, an application which displays the weekly updated scheduled roadworks and records of lane closures in England – useful for transport and logistical businesses. Other applications process information about health facilities and help families, friends, and affected people in their research. The 'Care Home Map', for example, allows to break down on the one side different care types such as dementia, physical disability, old age, or alcohol addiction, and matches them with local areas. Care Home Map also makes it easy to compare two facilities directly as it displays their ratings over time in order to see trends and differences in their quality – here information that was already available but needed elaborate research has been newly matched to inform the public. Other applications make use of statistical information on certain areas, for example, crime statistics useful for social workers, urban planners, or people who want to move. Admittedly these type of data needs to be treated with caution. How to capture the security of a place, for example, is one of the difficult questions in crime mapping. While frequent police patrols surely are part of making an area safer, their presence also increases the rate of criminal offences. Here the UK Crime Stats chose a rather direct approach. It not only ranked each neighbourhood among the most safe and most violent areas of the country, but it also listed the type of crime.

DOI: 10.1057/9781137373502

The 'Asborometer' application, on the other hand, simply maps out the Anti Social Behaviour orders of specific neighbourhoods. To the great displeasure of estate agents, this measurement of civil orders given in case of drug abuse, noise, or malicious communication among others, made it when first published in the TopTen of UK's iTunes App Store downloads. That citizens have an interest in dealing with data is also apparent as statistics are not only provided by the state, but are also collected by the citizens themselves. Here, websites and applications such as FixMyTransport and FixMyStreet detect existing problems to call the government or the public into account.

Interestingly, the application of digital platforms as a new form of civil participation comes with a dilemma. While computer skills – coding a platform – enable a new and different form of participation, they also raise a new issue: people who can program an application can draw the focus to a particular problem, while people without programming skills are disadvantaged in making themselves heard. A political dilemma. Back in Habermas times, the political public was an audience, whose role was first to critically observe. While the public's reflective and passive position as an audience has been discussed as a problem, it also had an equalizing effect: being informed by the news put everyone in the same state of knowledge. The algorithms of the digital public, on the other hand, offer a much more direct form of participation. The digital public actively takes part in the technical ensemble, but this questions the equalizing effect, and the new plurality triggered by active participation is challenged by a digital divide.

Paradoxically, participation splinters the public – the fragmentation of digitalization doesn't spare publicness. Raw data sets, for example, are of use to developers, but of no use to the general public. This situation, however, doesn't pose a new dilemma. Like Lawrence Lessig (2000) once rightly argued, code has a certain similarity to laws: Their judicial text is made for all of us, even though only lawyers can understand what exactly is talked about. In a digital era, establishing equality among their people is therefore again an important government task. In our past, education has played a central role to ensure a broad political participation and enable social mobility disregarding our differences. In our present, we have to find a balance between the new plurality of participation and equal opportunities, too. An elaborate task, which also will need dedicated resources. For everyone should know how to use the internet; not everyone needs to be able to program an application for a mobile phone, but for an equal chance everyone should be able to learn it. Experts in community informatics

DOI: 10.1057/9781137373502

such as Michael Gurstein (2008) recommend tackling the problem of data exclusion with a public investment in tools which help to lower the technical barrier for the normal citizen. The US Department of Labor, for example, has indeed answered with the launch of an interface project for tools to help programming an application. The outcome of the structural transformation of the public, however, is twofold. As we have seen above, it affects the public. But it also affects the citizen.

When Habermas defined the citizen in the sense of an audience, it had the duty to critically observe, and this quite passive approach was bound by a structural condition: before digitalization, to support an issue or cause had to be done by financial aid or voluntary work. This often meant giving part of your working time, which was difficult in a society characterized by full time employment. Here, digital communication allows a far more detailed management of affairs which is restructuring the political and social sphere. In our pre-digital past, little help – the bank transfer of £2 on paper, for example – would have caused an administrative problem and not much help. In the digital era, algorithms assist and automatize administration. Due to their work, small amounts of given time and money don't threaten to occupy an organization anymore. This means that participation can be coordinated to a new extent, and regardless of time and money, everyone can add his or her support – one can start to see that the rise of a new technical ensemble also might have interesting political implications. Potentially, digital technology can trigger a shift from a *representative* to a *participatory democracy* that probably would have fascinated a political philosopher such as Hannah Arendt. As we will see in the next section, this transformation of organization will spread further to allow humans not only to communicate but also integrate things. In effect, the emerging 'internet of things' can restructure our society in such a fundamental way that we can concede a silent revolution. If this revolution will take a promising turn and change our societies for the better, it can't be taken for granted. As we have seen with the spreading of 'networks' (Thacker and Galloway 2007; Morozov 2011), technology doesn't guarantee equal societies. But when aiming for them, it can be of use.

The internet of things

In the past, to pursue a large-scale organization has been reserved for states and multinational corporations. Could it be that soon the field

DOI: 10.1057/9781137373502

of organization will face the same disruption as the field of publishing before? In the beginning of mass digitalization, we saw that some blogs became relevant enough to influence and compete with traditional news organizations. In this chapter, I aim to show that the internet of things provides a similar potential with interesting political implications. For this, the technological principles, on which the internet of things is built, will be introduced, followed by a quick evaluation of areas in which the technology is currently discussed. From there, the text turns to the technology's social potential.

The technological ground of 'the internet of things' is already laid out; it generally refers to the digital organization of uniquely identifiable objects or devices. Its technical backbone was made up of the combination of several technical developments, of which the following three introduce the basic idea:

1 The rise of internet enabled devices: more and more objects and devices connect to the digital sphere on a mass market scale. A study by the European Commission estimates that by the year 2020 the 'internet of PCs' will have transformed into an 'internet of things' with 50 to 100 billion connected devices (Sundmaeker et al. 2010, 3).

2 The application of chips to a mass of mundane objects: technology such as the wireless communication RFID has reached the mass market with its low production costs; it can use the reading device as a power supply. RFID tags have been implemented in passports or credit cards early on, and show a high potential of being further minimalized. In 2007 Hitachi developed a chip measuring 0.05 mm, and in 2009 the Bristol University successfully glued RFID micro-transponders to live ants in order to study their behaviour.

3 The switch to a new internet protocol: The version IPv6 offers a large address space with 3.4×10^{38} unique addresses, enough to attach an address to all the objects that surround us individually – according to estimations we interact with 5,000 objects daily. It is a 128-bit address in eight 16-bit blocks which has the format global:subnet:interface and looks, for example, like this: FE80:000 0:0000:0000:0202:B3FF:FE1E:7329. It can also be written in a form that collapses the zeros.

Combining these different innovations, it will soon be possible to equip countless objects with digital tags, which then can be connected to the

DOI: 10.1057/9781137373502

internet and communicated with. Remote communication is on the rise – some of these digital tags can transfer the information without requiring a line of sight. The computer scientist Mark Weiser known for coining the term 'ubiquitous computing' was one of the first to envision computers as a pervasive part of everyday life. While his idea for the computer was still the 'intelligent agent' (Weiser 1991), the smart objects are more of an ambient intelligence, responsive but not really an agent. Their potential lies in the network. It will be their connections and not an agent that could potentially make a difference.

In the humanities, this potential has earlier been spotted and discussed. Katherine Hayles noticed: 'The challenge RFID presents is how to use it to re-think human subjectivity in constructive and life-enhancing ways without capitulating to its coercive and exploitive aspects' (2009, 48). Likewise Jordan Crandall (2011) sees with the internet of things the possibility of a new combinatory agency rising, which he describes in his comprehensive text as a participatory dimension relying on 'citizen activated sensors'. And when thinking about human agency and meaning in information-intensive environments, Nigel Thrift came to a similar conclusion. It reads as sympathetic as radical: 'If things are showing up differently, we can do different things too, energetically opening up the new order of being' (Thrift 2004, 188). Like Matthew Fuller (2005), they all point out that those smart objects will fundamentally revolutionize our 'media ecology' in one way or another: they will surely shift the 'massive and dynamic interrelation of processes and objects, beings and things, patterns and matter' (2005, 2) further. With Simondon we can say, we experience the rise of a new technical ensemble. What is its potential? Will it lead to a different 'technical reality'? Is the becoming of a different world concealed in this readdressing of it? What could the mechanisms of this different world be?

Besides some visionary thinkers in the humanities, economic organizations are excited to address the 'internet of things' as the icing on the cake of their digitalization. Companies such as General Electric (2013) proclaim the rise of an 'industrial internet'. IBM (2013) has launched the corporate initiative 'Smarter Planet' to explore smart grids, water management systems, and traffic control. Google (2013), besides developing Google Glass, tests a self-driving car. But the internet of things also comes with an even more groundbreaking social potential, because its automation of organization is freeing resources in a much broader scale. To get an idea of the social potential of this new technical ensemble as

DOI: 10.1057/9781137373502

well as to understand its 'technology of power' (see Chapter 3), however, we need to take a look at the current status of social organization.

According to media theorist Ned Rossiter, social organizations are not in a good state. Studying our contemporary network societies and information-based economies, he found that social organizations haven't really made use of the internet's disruptive potential. The internet, so his analyses, had mostly been incorporated by existing organizations which became 'networked organizations'. He describes those as follows: 'the networked organization is distinguished by its standing reserve of capital and its exploitation of the potentiality of labour-power. Such institutions are motivated by the need to organize social relations in the hope of maximizing "creativity" and regenerating the design of commodity forms that have long reached market saturation' (Rossiter 2006, 206–207). However, he also sees the potential for a 'new institutional actant' (209), a different form of organization he calls 'organized networks'. Here, 'information flows and social-technical relations are organized around site-specific projects' as they 'place an emphasis on process as the condition of outcomes' (207). Like the networked organization, the structure of an organized network is based on connections, but it operates these connections with a fundamentally different orientation or 'orchestration' (205). As the emphasis of the project is put more on *process* than on *success*, we don't find capital or profit in its centre. Its process is built on social-technical relations – to a certain extent we can say, Rossiter describes the structure of a new 'technical ensemble'. Indeed, we find his thoughts built with Simondon's words: 'The organized network carries the potential for the individuation of subjectivities into new institutional forms. This process is one of political invention' (210). And this process might be already well on its way.

In the industrial age, large-scale organizations had to be implemented by an equivalently large institution. In our Western societies, the financial budget defines the size of a project. Social organizations are very aware of this. The Red Cross, Greenpeace, Amnesty International, or Water Aid, all share a very well visible 'donate online' button. More money means more social services. When public service, social organizations, or other institutions manage workers, buildings, things in often lengthy and costly processes, it is money which makes something happen. Digital technology, however, makes it much easier to manage a large-scale project, and its capacity will evolve with the internet of things. This could potentially reduce their dependency on money. In education, already two projects

DOI: 10.1057/9781137373502

anticipate the potential and possible change this could introduce. They give us a glimpse where the internet of things may take our societies, when instead of buying things needed for a project, the necessary elements can be directly connected.

Up till now, the administration of our schools and colleges had been quite difficult: from the building manager to the teacher, from rooms to tools, from laboratories to gyms, from canteens to last but not least pupils, everything had to be coordinated. It was costly, and a difficult problem. Sometimes rooms were double booked, while at other times the whole building was empty – most evenings for example. However, re-distributing resources in a different way could open up new chances. Martha Lane Fox, an inspiring entrepreneur, who had successfully co-founded the travel start-up lastminute.com, decided in 2009 to launch the non-profit project 'Race Online 2012'. Its aim was to tackle the digital divide in Britain, in order to raise awareness and help the 14 million Britons who hadn't been online at that time; most of them among the socially most disadvantaged. In tackling that problem, her project took an innovative approach. Its website didn't ask just for money. Instead, the original website of 'RaceOnline 2012' (the project was ended in 2012) used the web to gather rooms, material, skills, working time – and also asked for money, but just among those other things. On this webpage, the donate-button wasn't the first thing that caught your eye. Its complex, yet elegant interface design asked users to let the organization know in great detail at what time in the week rooms in their office were available, or which timeslot one would be free each week for teaching, and if one would be convenient with teaching groups or would prefer one-to-one tuition.

The approach of the 'Public School' is similar. Its autodidactic experiment starts with the proposition of classes on the Public School's website: I want to teach the following or learn the following. If enough people are interested and sign up to a class, a rotating committee decides when the classes can be scheduled and finds a teacher. The project was originally initiated by Telic Arts Exchange in Los Angeles in 2008, and has branches in Berlin, Brussels, San Juan, Helsinki, New York, and Philadelphia. The Berlin school offers, for example, the seminars 'Arabic for Beginners', 'Wittgenstein', 'Practicalities of Revolt', 'Soviet Cinema', or a seminar on 'The Possibility of Digitally Committing Suicide on Social Media Platforms'. While the Obama campaign was equally run on money and people's power, here – again very different to other social

DOI: 10.1057/9781137373502

aid projects – money isn't what you are asked for. Instead these projects make use of the digital potential to coordinate needs more directly. The projects even might still have a financial budget but the logic of money fades from the spotlight. They are *non-money centred organizations*, and use the network in Rossiter's sense, which is why the financial budget isn't defining anymore the size and extent of their enterprise.

Both projects are exemplary for something that will exceed education: the force of a project once released by money can now also be released by technology: new connections allow things to show up differently. How to make further use of the ability of this internet of things, to aggregate and mashup solutions to social issues is already discussed. The Social Innovation Camp, among other projects, tests, for example, how to apply the technique of hacking to the world, in order to prototype parts of a new society in the shell of the old (McQuillan 2012). Digitalization has disrupted our societies before with its ability to skip the intermediaries. What, if this intermediary is money? In our industrial past, the machines suitable for serial production had been capital-intensive. With the rise of computers, entrepreneurs suddenly have affordable, multifaceted means of production at their hands – one reason why the term 'New Economy' was coined. In this economy, the success of a company depends as much on investment capital as on a brilliant idea; at least for a while. Now digitalization offers another revolutionizing potential: via digital means money isn't at the centre of a project. Due to digitalization, money might become again a means among others; and demands can get organized via social-technical connections directly. A potential of digital organization that will be further set free with the internet of things – with it the chance for a 'non-state-run public sphere' (Virno 2006) emerges. One can organize an enterprise which doesn't need to function according to a financial logic. Instead, the idea of a scientific, creative, informational, enlightening, playful, poetic, political, or entrepreneurial project is the focus, and not the question of money or profit. Money can again become a means among others, but not an end in itself. Which is about time. In the midst of the twentieth century, the economic historian Karl Polanyi had noticed (1944, 81) that the market and its economic logic, once nothing but an appendage of our societies, was about to become the new religion. The economic discourse of the free market had challenged the political system by presenting itself as a critique of governmental reason, claiming that nobody can know the totality of the economic process, and therefore rule it, not even a democratic parliament. 'There is no

DOI: 10.1057/9781137373502

sovereign in economics' (Foucault 2008, 283). Only this doesn't mean that economics is the sovereign either. Today, there is again a need for spheres that function according to an own and different logic than the economic one. Due to digitalization, these projects and enterprises can be quite factual.

Aiming for change, contemporary opposition means to organize what before could only be preached. The outcome might just be a necessary balance to an economy which has become a superpower; it could also erect a new world crosswise in the existing. Change isn't necessarily loud and realized at one blow – when Walter Benjamin thought about alienated life, he pondered the idea of a virtual yet crucial shift that will not 'change the world by force but will merely make a slight adjustment in it' (Benjamin 1934, 811). Money will not vanish like a face drawn in the sand at the edge of the sea, but that doesn't mean it will be at the centre of our human societies forever. Digitalization allows us to create a different future. It will become what we make of it.

DOI: 10.1057/9781137373502

References

Adorno, Theodor W. and Horkheimer, Max [1944] 2002, *Dialectic of Enlightenment*, Stanford, University Press.

Amirault, Ray J. and Branson, Robert K. 2006, 'Educators and Expertise: A Brief History of Theories and Models', in *The Cambridge Handbook of Expertise and Expert Performance*, edited by K. Anders Ericsson et al., Cambridge, Cambridge University Press, 69–86.

Anderson, Chris 2006, *The Long Tail: How Endless Choice Is Creating Unlimited Demand*, London, Business Books.

Arendt, Hannah [1958] 1998, *The Human Condition*, Chicago, University of Chicago.

Arendt, Hannah [1967] 2000, 'Truth and Politics', in *The Portable Hannah Arendt*, edited by Peter Baehr, London, Penguin, 545–575.

Arendt, Hannah 2005, *The Promise of Politics*, New York, Random House.

Aristotle 2003, 'On "Techne" and "Episteme"', in *Philosophy of Technology. The Technological Condition. An Anthology*, edited by Scharff, Robert C. and Dusek, Val, Oxford, Blackwell, 19–24.

Auerbach, Erich [1953] 2003, *Mimesis: The Representation of Reality in Western Literature*, translated by Willard Trask, Princeton University Press.

Barbrook, Richard and Cameron, Andy 1996, 'The Californian Ideology', *Science as Culture*, 6/1, 44–72.

BBC 2013a, 'JK Rowling Crime Book Cuckoo's Calling Sees Sales Boost', available at <http://www.bbc.co.uk/news/entertainment-arts-23430857>, [accessed 1 October 2013].

DOI: 10.1057/9781137373502

BBC 2013b, 'Guidelines. Section 7. Privacy and Consent', available at <http://www.bbc.co.uk/editorialguidelines/page/guidelines-privacy-privacy-consent>, [accessed 1 October 2013].

Beckmann, Johann [1777] 1809, *Anleitung zur Technologie oder zur Kentniss der Handwerke, Fabriken und Manufacturen, vornehmlich derer, die mit der Landwirthschaft, Polizey und Cameralwissenschaft in nächster Verbindung stehn*, Göttingen.

Bell, Daniel 1974, *The Coming of Post-Industrial Society: A Venture in Social Forecasting*, London, Heinemann.

Benjamin, Walter [1927] 1999, 'Moscow', in *Selected Writings Volume 1, 1927–1934*, edited by Marcus Bullock and Michael W. Jennings, translated by Rodney Livingstone and others, Cambridge MA, Harvard University Press, 22–46.

Benjamin, Walter [1928] 2009, *One-Way Street and Other Writings*, translated by Edmund Jephcott and Kingsley Shorter, London, Penguin.

Benjamin, Walter [1934] 2005, 'Franz Kafka', in *Selected Writings Volume 2, 1931–1934*, edited by Marcus Bullock and Michael W. Jennings, translated by Rodney Livingstone and others, Cambridge MA, Harvard University Press, 794–819.

Benjamin, Walter [1936] 1972, 'Pariser Brief [1]: Gide und sein neuer Gegner', in *Gesammelte Schriften*, edited by Walter Benjamin, Band III, Frankfurt am Main: Suhrkamp, 483–495.

Berardi, Franco 2009, *The Soul at Work: From Alienation to Autonomy*, Los Angeles, Semiotext(e), Cambridge MA, MIT Press.

Berardi, Franco 2013, *The Uprising: On Poetry and Finance*, Los Angeles, Semiotext(e), Cambridge MA, MIT Press.

Berry, David 2011, *The Philosophy of Software: Code and Mediation in the Digital Age*, London, Palgrave Macmillan.

Berry, David 2012, *Understanding Digital Humanities*, London: Palgrave Macmillan.

Blumenberg, Hans 2009, *Geistesgeschichte der Technik*, Frankfurt am Main, Suhrkamp.

Boltanski, Luc and Chiapello, Eve 2005, *The New Spirit of Capitalism*, translated by Gregory Elliott, London, New York, Verso.

Bosse, Heinrich 1990, 'Der geschärfte Befehl zum Selbstdenken. Ein Erlaß des Ministers v. Fürst an die preußischen Universitäten im Mai 1770', in *Diskursanalysen 2. Institution Universität*, edited by Friedrich Adolf Kittler, Manfred Schneider, and Samuel Weber, Opladen, Westdeutscher Verlag, 31–62.

DOI: 10.1057/9781137373502

Breheim, D. J. 1961, ' "Open Shop" Programming at Rocketdyne Speeds
    Research and Production', *Computers and Automation*, 10, July, 8–9.
Brendon, Piers 1991, *Thomas Cook: 150 Years of Popular Tourism*, London,
    Secker & Warburg.
Brin, Sergey and Page, Lawrence 1998, 'The Anatomy of Large-Scale
    Hypertextual Web Search Engine', available at <http://infolab.
    stanford.edu/~backrub/google.html>, [accessed 1 October 2013].
Broom, Alex and Adams, Jon 2010, 'The Reconfiguration of Expertise
    in Oncology: The Practice of Prediction and Articulation of
    Indeterminacy in Medical Consultations', *Qualitative Health Research*,
    October 2010, 20/10, 1433–1445.
Brynjolfsson, Erik and Hu, Yu Jeffrey and Smith, Michael D. 2006,
    'From Niches to Riches: Anatomy of the Long Tail', *Sloan Management
    Review*, 47/4, 67–71.
Brynjolfsson, Erik and McAfee, Andre 2011, *Race Against the Machine:
    How the Digital Revolution Is Accelerating Innovation, Driving
    Productivity, and Irreversibly Transforming Employment and the
    Economy*, Lexington Massachusetts, Digital Frontier Press.
Bunz, Mercedes 2010, 'In the US, Algorithms Are Already Reporting
    the News', in *The Guardian*, 30. March 2010, available at <http://www.
    theguardian.com/media/pda/2010/mar/30/digital-media-algorithms-
    reporting-journalism> [accessed 1 October 2013].
Bunz, Mercedes 2012a, 'As You Like It: Critique in the Era of an
    Affirmative Discourse', in *The Unlike Us Reader, Social Media
    Monopolies and Their Alternatives*, edited by Geert Lovink and Miriam
    Rasch, Amsterdam, Institute of Network Cultures, 137–145.
Bunz, Mercedes 2012b, 'Das offene Geheimnis. Zur Politik der Wahrheit
    im Datenjournalismus', in *Wikileaks und die Folgen. Netz – Medien –
    Politik*, edited by Heinrich Geiselberger, Berlin, Suhrkamp, 134–151.
Bunz, Mercedes 2013, 'The Power of Information: A Journey Back in
    Time to the Faultlines of Globalization, Art, and Media in the Early
    1990s', in *The Whole Earth Catalogue*, edited by Diedrich Diederichsen
    and Anselm Franke, Berlin, 172–176.
Bush, Corlann Gee 1983, 'Women and the Assessment of Technology:
    To Think, to Be; to Unthink, to Free', in *Machina Ex Dea: Feminist
    Perspectives on Technology*, edited by Joan Rothschild, New York,
    Pergamon Press, 151–170.
Canetti, Elias [1960] 2000, *Crowds and Power*, translated by Victor
    Gollancz, London, Phoenix Press.

DOI: 10.1057/9781137373502

Carr, David 2009, 'The Robots Are Coming! Oh, They're Here', *The New York Times*, 19. October 2009, available at <http://mediadecoder. blogs.nytimes.com/2009/10/19/the-robots-are-coming-oh-theyre-here> [accessed 1 October 2013].

Carr, David 2010, 'Not Creating It; Just Protecting It', *The New York Times*, 29, March 2010, B1.

Carr, Nicholas 2008, 'Is Google Making Us Stupid', *The Atlantic Monthly*, July 2008, available at <http://www.theatlantic.com/magazine/ archive/2008/07/is-google-making-us-stupid/6868/>, [accessed 1 October 2013].

Carr, Nicholas 2010, *The Shallows. How the Internet Is Changing the Way We Think, Read and Remember*, London, Atlantic Books.

Cheney-Lippold, John 2011, 'A New Algorithmic Identity: Soft Biopolitics and the Modulation of Control', *Theory, Culture & Society*, 28, 6, 164–181.

Chun, Wendy 2008, 'On "Sourcery", or Code as Fetish', *Configurations*, 16/3, Fall, 299–324.

Chun, Wendy 2013, *Programmed Visions: Software and Memory*, Cambridge MA, MIT Press.

Coleman, Gabriella 2013, *Coding Freedom: The Ethics and Aesthetics of Hacking*, Princeton University Press.

Combes, Muriel 2013, *Gilbert Simondon and the Philosophy of the Transindividual*, translated by Thomas LaMarre, Cambridge MA, MIT Press.

Cormen, Thomas H. 2013, *Algorithms Unlocked*, Cambridge MA, MIT Press.

Crandall, Jordan 2011, 'Movement, Agency and Sensing in "Cognitive Architecture"', available at <http://www.jordancrandall.com/ main/+writings/CogArch.pdf>, [accessed 1 October 2013].

Croll, Alistair and Yoskovitz, Benjamin 2013, *Lean Analytics: Use Data to Build a Better Startup Faster*, Sebastopol, O'Reilly Media.

Dean, Jodi 2009, *Democracy and Other Neoliberal Fantasies, Communicative Capitalism and Left Politics*, Duke University Press.

De Boever, Arne, Murray, Alex, Roffe, Jon and Woodward, Ashley (eds) 2013, *Gilbert Simondon. Being and Technology*, Edinburgh University Press.

Deleuze, Gilles [1966] 2001, 'Review of Gilbert Simondon's L'individu et sa genèse physico-biologique (1966)', *Pli* 12, translated by Ivan Ramirez, 43–49.

DOI: 10.1057/9781137373502

Deleuze, Gilles and Guattari, Félix [1980] 1993, *A Thousand Plateaus*, translated by Brian Massumi, University of Minnesota.

Dingman, Maurice 1958, ex informata conscientia (letter), available at <http://www.bishop-accountability.org/ia-davenport/archives/jnw-ex-19-J-57.pdf>, [accessed 1 October 2013].

Divine, Robert A. 1993, *The Sputnik Challenge*, Oxford University Press.

Domingos, Pedro 2012, 'A Few Useful Things to Know about Machine Learning', *Communications of the ACM*, 55/10, 78–87.

Dreyfus, Hubert L. 1972, *What Computers Can't Do: A Critique of Artificial Reason*. New York, Harper & Row.

Driscoll, Kevin 2012, 'From Punchcards to "Big Data": A History of Database Populism', *communication +1*, 1/4, available at http://scholarworks.umass.edu/cpo/vol1/iss1/4, [accessed 1 October 2013].

Düttmann, Alexander Garcìa 2007, *Philosophy of Exaggeration*, London, New York, Continuum.

Ehrenberg, Alain 2009, *Weariness of the Self: Diagnosing the History of Depression in the Contemporary Age*, Montreal, McGill-Queen's University Press.

Eisenstein, Elizabeth 1979, *The Printing Press as an Agent of Change*, Cambridge University Press.

Ernst, Wolfgang 2012, *Digital Memory and the Archive*, Minnesota University Press.

Fisch, Karl 2006, 'Did you know?' [online], available at <http://thefischbowl.blogspot.com/2006/08/did-you-know.html>, [accessed 1 October 2013].

Florida, Richard 2002, *The Rise of the Creative Class and How It Is Transforming Work, Leisure, Community and Everyday Life*, New York, Basic Books.

Foucault, Michel [1961] 1965, *Madness and Civilization*, translated by R. Howard. London, Tavistock.

Foucault, Michel [1975] 1977, *Discipline and Punish: The Birth of the Prison*, translated by Alan Sheridan, New York, Pantheon Books.

Foucault, Michel 1998, 'The Order of the Discourse', in *Untying The Text. A Post-Structuralist Reader*, edited by Robert Young, London, Routledge, 51–78.

Foucault, Michel 2007, *Security, Territory, Population: Lectures at the College de France. 1977–1978*, London, Palgrave MacMillan.

Foucault, Michel 2008, *The Birth of Biopolitics: Lectures at the College de France. 1978–1979*, London, Palgrave MacMillan.

DOI: 10.1057/9781137373502

Freud, Sigmund [1921] 2004, 'Mass Psychology and Analysis of the "I" ', in *Mass Psychology and Other Writings*, edited by Sigmund Freud and translated by J. A. Underwood, London, Penguin Classics.

Fuller, Matthew 2003, *Behind the Blip: Essays on the Culture of Software*, New York, Autonomedia.

Fuller, Matthew 2005, *Media Ecologies: Materialist Energies in Art and Technoculture*, Cambridge MA, MIT Press.

Fuller, Matthew (ed.) 2008, *Software Studies: A Lexicon*, Cambridge MA, MIT Press.

Fuller, Matthew and Goffey, Andrew 2012, *Evil Media*, Cambridge MA, MIT Press.

Gans, Herbert 1979, *Deciding What's News: A Study of CBS Evening News, NBC Nightly News, Newsweek and Time*, New York, Pantheon Books.

Galloway, Alexander 2004, *Protocol – How Control Exists after Decentralisation*, Cambridge MA, MIT Press.

Gao, Huiji, Barbier, Geoffrey and Goolsby, Rebecca (2011) 'Harnessing the Crowdsourcing Power of Social Media for Disaster Relief', *Intelligent Systems, IEEE*, 26/3, 10–14.

Gehlen, Arnold [1957] 1980, *Man in the Age of Technology*, Columbia University Press.

Giddens Anthony 1994, 'Living in a Post-Traditional Society', in *Reflexive Modernization, Politics, Tradition and Aesthetics in the Modern Social Order*, edited by Ulrich Beck, Anthony Giddens and Scott Lash, Polity Press, Cambridge, 56–109.

Goffey, Andrew 2008, 'Algorithm', in *Software Studies: A Lexicon*, edited by Matthew Fuller, Cambridge MA, MIT Press, 15–20.

Grier, David Alan 2005, *When Computers Were Human*, Princeton University Press.

Gurstein, Michael 2008, *What Is Community Informatics (and Why Does It Matter)?* Monza, Polimetrica.

Habermas, Jürgen [1962] 1989, *The Structural Transformation of the Public Sphere*, translated by Thomas Burger, Cambridge MA, MIT Press.

Habermas, Jürgen [1968] 1971, 'Technology and Science as "Ideology" ', in *Toward a Rational Society; Student Protest, Science, and Politics*, edited by Jürgen Habermas, Boston, Beacon Press, 81–122.

Haraway, Donna J. 1997, *Modest_Witness@Second_Millenium. FemaleMan©_Meets_OncoMouseTM, Feminism and Technoscience*, New York, London, Routledge.

DOI: 10.1057/9781137373502

Hardt, Michael and Negri, Antonio 2000, *Empire*, Cambridge MA, Harvard University Press.

Hardt, Michael and Negri, Antonio 2004, *Multitude: War and Democracy in the Age of Empire*, New York, Penguin Press.

Harvey, David 2005, *A Brief History of Neoliberalism*, Oxford University Press.

Hayles, Katherine N. 2009, 'RFID – Human Agency and Meaning in Information-Intensive Environments', *Theory, Culture & Society*, 26, 47–72.

Hayles, Katherine N. 2012, *How We Think: Digital Media and Contemporary Technogenesis*, Chicago University Press.

Heidegger, Martin [1927] 1962, *Being and Time*, translated by John Macquarrie and Edward Robinson, Oxford Blackwell.

Heidegger, Martin [1954] 1977, *'The Question Concerning Technology' and other essays*, translated by William Lovitt, New York, London, Harper & Row.

Heidegger, Martin 1982, *Die Technik und Die Kehre*, Pfullingen, Neske.

Herd, Harold 1927, *The Making of Modern Journalism*, London, Allen & Unwin Ltd.

Herd, Harold 1952, *The March of Journalism: The Story of the British Press from 1622 to the Present Day*, London, Allen & Unwin Ltd.

Hui, Yuk 2012, 'What Is a Digital Object?' *Metaphilosophy*, 43, 380–395, available at <doi: 10.1111/j.1467–9973.2012.01761.x>

Idle, Nadia and Nunns, Alex 2011, *Tweets from Tahrir: Egypt's Revolution as It Unfolded, in the Words of the People Who Made It*, New York, OR Books.

Ihde, Don 1979, *Technics and Praxis*, Dordrecht, Reidel.

Ihde, Don 1990, *Technology and the Lifeworld*, Bloomington, Indiana University Press.

Illouz, Eva 2007, *Cold Intimacies: The Making of Emotional Capitalism*, Cambridge, Polity Press

Intelligent Information Laboratory 2010, 'Stats Monkey' [online], available at <http://infolab.northwestern.edu/projects/stats-monkey/>, [accessed 1 October 2013].

Jarvie, I. C. [1967] 1983, 'Technology and the Structure of Knowledge', in *Philosophy and Technology. Readings in the philosophical problems of technology*, edited by Carl Mitcham, Robert Mackey, London, Palgrave Macmillan, Free Press, 54–61.

DOI: 10.1057/9781137373502

Jarvis, Jeff 2011, *Public Parts: How Sharing in the Digital Age Improves the Way We Work and Live*, New York, Simon & Schuster.

Jefferson, Thomas [1787] 1955, 'Letter to Edward Carrington on the 16 January 1787', in *The Papers of Thomas Jefferson, Volume 11: 1 January to 6 August 1787*, edited by Julian P. Boyd, Princeton University Press, 48–49.

Kant, Immanuel [1787] 2009, *An Answer to the Question: What Is Enlightenment?* London, Penguin.

Kant, Immanuel [1790] 2007, *Critique of Judgment*, translated by James Creed Meredith, Oxford University Press.

Kapp, Ernst 1877, *Grundlinien einer Philosophie der Technik. Zur Entstehungsgeschichte der Cultur aus neuen Gesichtspunkten*, Braunschweig, Georg Westermann.

Kelly, Kevin 2010, *What Technology Wants*, London, Penguin.

Kenski, Kate, Hardy, Bruce W. and Jamieson, Kathleen Hall 2010, *The Obama Victory: How Media, Money, and Message Shaped the 2008 Election*, Oxford University Press.

Kitchin, Frederick Harcourt 1925, *Moberly Bell and His Times: An Unofficial Narrative*, London, P. Allen & Co.

Kittler, Friedrich 1995, 'There Is No Software', *ctheory* 10/18, available at http://www.ctheory.net/articles.aspx?id=74>, [accessed 1. October 2013].

Kittler, Friedrich 2009, 'Towards an Ontology of Media', *Theory, Culture & Society*, 26/(2–3), 23–31.

Kjaer, Poul F., Teubner, Gunther and Febbrajo, Alberto 2011, *The Financial Crisis in Constitutional Perspective: The Dark Side of Functional Differentiation*, Oxford, Hart.

Krakauer, Jon 1997, *Into Thin Air: Personal Account of the Everest Disaster*, New York, Villard.

Kroker, Arthur 1994, *Data Trash: The Theory of the Virtual Class*, New York, St. Martin's Press.

Kurzweil, Ray 1999, *The Age of Spiritual Machines: When Computers Exceed Human Intelligence*, New York, Viking.

LaMarre, Thomas 2013, 'Afterword: Humans and Machines', in *Gilbert Simondon and the Philosophy of the Transindividual*, edited by Muriel Combes, Cambridge MA, MIT Press, 79–108.

Lanchester, John 2012, 'Marx at 193', *London Review of Books*, 34/7, 5 April, 7–10.

DOI: 10.1057/9781137373502

Lanier, Jaron 2010, *You Are Not a Gadget: A Manifesto*, New York, Alfred A. Knopf.

Lanier, Jaron 2013, *Who Owns the Future?* London, Penguin, Allen Lane.

Lash, Scott 2002, *Critique of Information*, London, Sage Publications.

Latour, Bruno 1999, *Pandora's Hope: Essays on the Reality of Science Studies*, Harvard, University Press.

Lazzarato, Maurizio 1997, *Lavoro immateriale. Forme di vita e produzione di soggettività*, Verona, Ombre Corte.

Le Bon, Gustave [1894] 1995, *The Crowd: A Study of the Popular Mind*, London, Transaction.

Leibniz, Gottfried-Wilhelm 1951, 'The Art of Discovery (1685)', in *Leibniz, Selections*, edited by Philip P. Wiener, New York, Charles Scribener's Sons, 50–58.

Leroi-Gourhan, André [1964] 1993, *Gesture and Speech*, translated by Anna Bostock Berger, Cambridge MA, MIT Press.

Lessig, Lawrence 2000, *Code and Other Laws of Cyberspace*, New York, Basic Books.

Levenhus, Abbey 2010, 'Online Relationship Management in a Presidential Campaign: A Case Study of the Obama Campaign's Management of Its Internet-Integrated Grassroots Effort', *Journal of Public Relations Research*, 22/3, 313–335.

Lippmann, Walter (ed.) 1920, 'Journalism and the Higher Law', in *Liberty and the News*, New York, Harcourt, Brace and Howe, 3–17.

Liu, Alan 2012, 'Where Is Cultural Criticism in the Digital Humanities?' in *Debates in the Digital Humanities*, edited by Mathew K. Gold, University of Minnesota Press, 490–509.

Lovink, Geert 2007, *Zero Comments, Blogging and Critical Internet Culture*, London, Routledge.

Lovink, Geert 2012, *Networks Without a Cause: A Critique of Social Media*, Cambridge, Malden, Polity Press.

Lucas, Rob 2012, 'The Critical Net Critic', *New Left Review*, 77, September/October, 45–69.

Lucchetti, Aaron and Philbin, Brett 2012, 'Now, It Is Man vs. Machine. As Morgan Stanley Beefs up Bond Business, Firm Is Bringing in More Computers', *The Wall Street Journal*, 9. August 2012, p. C1; available at <http://online.wsj.com/article/SB1000 0872396390443991704577577190049118980.html>, [accessed 1. October 2013].

DOI: 10.1057/9781137373502

Lunenfeld, Peter, Burdick, Anne, Drucker, Johanna, Presner, Todd and Schnapp, Jeffrey 2012, *Digital_Humanities*, Cambridge MA, MIT Press.

Luo, Michael 2008, 'Study: Many Obama Small Donors Really Weren't', *The New York Times* 24.11.2008, available at <http://thecaucus.blogs.nytimes.com/2008/11/24/study-obamas-small-donors-really-werent/>, [accessed 1. October 2013].

Mackay, Charles [1841] 1995, *Extraordinary Popular Delusions and the Madness of Crowds*, Ware, Wordsworth Reference.

Malabou, Catherine 2008, *What Should We Do with Our Brain?* New York, Fordham University Press.

Malbin, Michael J. 2009, 'Small Donors, Large Donors and the Internet: The Case for Public Financing after Obama', *The Campaign Finance Institute*, available at <http://www.cfinst.org/Press/PReleases/08–11–24/Realty_Check_-_Obama_Small_Donors.aspx>, [accessed 1. October 2013].

Manovich, Lev 2013, *Software Takes Command*, London, Bloomsbury.

Marcuse, Herbert 1941, 'Some Social Implications of Modern Technology', *Studies in Philosophy and Social Science*, 9/3, 414–439.

Marinetti, Filippo Tommaso [1909] 1960, 'The Futurist Manifesto', in *Intellectuals in Politics: Three Biographical Essays – Léon Blum, Walther Rathenau, F. T. Marinetti*, edited by James Joll, London, Weidenfeld & Nicolson, 179–184.

Markoff, John 2011, 'Armies of Expensive Lawyers, Replaced by Cheaper Software', *The New York Times*, March 5, 2011, p. A1, available at <http://www.nytimes.com/2011/03/05/science/05legal.html>, [accessed 1. October 2013].

McLuhan, Marshall [1962] 2002, *The Gutenberg Galaxy: The Making of Typographic Man*, University of Toronto Press.

McQuillan, Dan 2012, 'Could Prototyping Be the New Policy? ', available at <http://www.guardian.co.uk/culture-professionals-network/culture-professionals-blog/2012/may/28/prototyping-replaces-policy-arts-culture>, [accessed 1. October 2013].

Mitcham, Carl and Mackey, Robert [1972] 1983, *Philosophy and Technology: Readings in the Philosophical Problems of Technology*, London, Palgrave Macmillan, Free Press.

Miyazaki, Shintaro 2012: 'Understanding Micro-Temporality in Computational Cultures', *Computational Culture – A Journal of Software Studies*, 28, September 2012, available at <http://

DOI: 10.1057/9781137373502

computationalculture.net/article/algorhythmics-understanding-micro-temporality-in-computational-cultures>, [accessed 1. October 2013].

Moretti, Franco 2005, *Graphs, Maps, Trees*, London, Verso.

Morley, Robin 2012, 'A New BBC Social Media Strategy for England', *BBC Academy College of Journalism*, 27. February 2012, available at <http://www.bbc.co.uk/blogs/blogcollegeofjournalism/posts/local_matters_a_new_bbc_social>, [accessed 1 October 2013].

Morozov, Evgeny 2011, *The Net Delusion: The Dark Side of Internet Freedom*, New York, Public Affairs.

Mouffe, Chantal 2000, *Deliberative Democracy or Agonistic Pluralism*, Reihe Politikwissenschaft, Volume 72, Institute for Advanced Studies, Vienna.

Murong, Xuecun 2009, *Leave Me Alone: A Novel of Chengdu*, London, Sydney, Allen & Unwin.

Negroponte, Nicholas 1995, *Being Digital*, London, Hodder & Stoughton.

Nichols, Nathan, Gandy, Lisa and Hammond, Kristian 2009, 'From Generating to Mining: Automatically Scripting Conversations Using Existing Online Sources' [paper], *ICWSM, The Association for the Advancement of Artificial Intelligence Press.*

Obama, Barack 2011, Remarks by the President in State of Union Address, 25 January, United States Capitol, Washington, D.C., available at <http://www.whitehouse.gov/the-press-office/2011/01/25/remarks-president-state-union-address>, [accessed 1. October 2013].

OECD 2013, 'Crisis squeezes income and puts pressure on inequality and poverty' [report], available at <www.oecd.org/els/soc/OECD2013-Inequality-and-Poverty-8p.pdf>, [accessed 1. October 2013].

Ofcom Communications Market Report 2010, available at <http://stakeholders.ofcom.org.uk/binaries/research/cmr/753567/CMR_2010_FINAL.pdf>, [accessed 1. October 2013].

Parikka, Jussi 2012, *What Is Media Archeology?* Cambridge, Polity Press.

Pariser, Eli 2011, *The Filter Bubble: What the Internet Is Hiding from You*, London, Viking.

Parisi, Luciana 2013, *Contagious Architecture, Computation, Aesthetics, and Space*, Cambridge MA, MIT Press.

Parry, Richard, '*Episteme* and *Techne*', in *The Stanford Encyclopedia of Philosophy*, edited by Edward N. Zalta, available at <http://plato.

DOI: 10.1057/9781137373502

stanford.edu/archives/fall2008/entries/episteme-techne/>, [accessed 1. October 2013].

Plato 2005, *Phaedrus*, London, Penguin Classics.

Polanyi, Karl [1944] 2001, *The Great Transformation: The Political and Economical Origins of Our Time*, Boston, Beacon Press.

Quigley, Muireann 2008, 'Directed Deceased Organ Donation: The Problem with Algorithmic Ethics', available at <www.ccels.cf.ac.uk/archives/issues/2008/quigley.pdf>, [accessed 1. October 2013].

Rheingold, Howard 2002, *Smart Mobs: The Next Social Revolution*, Cambridge, Massachusetts, Perseus.

Robin, Corey 2004, *Fear: The History of a Political Idea*, Oxford University Press.

Rogers, Richard 2013, *Digital Methods*, Cambridge MA, MIT Press.

Rosen, Jay 2010, 'The Afghanistan War Logs Released by Wikileaks, the World's First Stateless News Organization', 26 July, available at <http://archive.pressthink.org/2010/07/26/wikileaks_afghan.html>, [accessed 1. October 2013].

Rossiter, Ned 2006, *Organized Networks: Media Theory, Creative Labour, New Institutions*, Rotterdam, NAi Publishers, Institute of Network Cultures.

Rusbridger, Alan 2010, 'The Splintering of the Fourth Estate', available at <http://www.guardian.co.uk/commentisfree/2010/nov/19/open-collaborative-future-journalism, [accessed 1. October 2013].

Rusbridger, Alan 2011, 'Inside Julian Assange's War on Secrecy – Introduction', in *Inside Julian Assange's War on Secrecy*, edited by David Leigh and Luke Harding, London, Guardian Books, 1–12.

Ryle, Gilbert 1949, *The Concept of Mind*, London, Hutchinson.

Scharff, Robert C. and Dusek, Val 2003 (eds), *Philosophy of Technology: The Technological Condition. An Anthology*, Oxford, Blackwell.

Searle, John 1980, 'Minds, Brains and Programs', *Behavioral and Brain Sciences*, 3/3, 417–445.

Shirky, Clay 2008, *Here Comes Everybody. How Change Happens When People Come Together*, London, Allen Lane.

Shirky, Clay 2011, *Cognitive Surplus: Creativity and Generosity in a Connected Age*, London, Allen Lane.

Simondon, Gilbert [1958] 1989, *Du Mode d'Existence des Objets Techniques*, Paris Aubier Editions.

Simondon, Gilbert 1980, *On the Mode of Existence of Technical Objects*, translated by Ninian Mellamphy, University of Western Ontario.

DOI: 10.1057/9781137373502

Simondon, Gilbert 2005, *L'individuation à la lumière des notions de forme et d'information*, Éditions Jérôme Millon.

Simondon, Gilbert 2012, 'Technical Mentality', in *Gilbert Simondon. Being and Technology*, edited by De Boever, Arne, Murray, Alex, Roffe, Jon and Woodward, Ashley, Edinburgh University Press, 1–15.

Simpson, Joe 1988, *Touching the Void*, London, Jonathan Cape.

Skolimowski, Henryk [1966] 1983, 'The Structure of Thinking in Knowledge', in *Philosophy and Technology: Readings in the Philosophical Problems of Technology*, edited by Carl Mitcham and Robert Mackey, London, Palgrave Macmillan, Free Press, 42–49.

Stelter, Brian 2008, 'Finding Political News Online the Young Pass It On', *The New York Times*, 27, March, A1.

Stiegler, Bernard [2010] 2013, *What Makes Life Worth Living: On Pharmacology*, Cambridge, Polity Press.

Sundmaeker, Harald, Guillemin, Patrick, Friess, Peter and Woelfflé, Sylvie 2010, *Vision and Challenges for Realising the Internet of Things*, Brussels, European Commission – Information Society and Media DG.

Surowiecki, James 2004, *The Wisdom of Crowds: Why the Many Are Smarter Than the Few and How Collective Wisdom Shapes Business, Economies, Societies, and Nations*, London, Doubleday.

Susan, Blackmore 2000, *The Meme Machine*, Oxford University Press.

SwiftRiver 2013, An Ushahidi Platform [leaflet], available at <http://www.ushahidi.com/products/swiftriver-platform>, [accessed 1. October 2013].

Terranova, Tiziana 2004, *Network Culture: Politics for the Information Age*, London, Pluto Press.

Thacker, Eugene and Galloway, Alexander 2007, *Exploit: A Theory of Networks*, Minneapolis, University of Minnesota.

Thrift, Nigel 2004, 'Remembering the Technological Unconscious by Foregrounding Knowledges of Position', *Environment and Planning D: Society and Space*, 22/1, 175–190.

Turing, Alan M. 1936, 'On Computable Numbers, with an Application to the Entscheidungsproblem', *Proceedings of the London Mathematical Society*, 42/2, 230–265.

Turkle, Sherry 2011, *Alone Altogether: Why We Expect More from Technology and Less from Each Other*, New York, Basic Books.

US Department of State 2010, 'Department of State Launches New Tool to Foster Online Open Dialogue' [press release], available at

DOI: 10.1057/9781137373502

<http://www.state.gov/r/pa/prs/ps/2010/03/138326.htm>, [accessed 1 October 2013].

Vargas, Jose Antonio 2008, 'The Clickocracy: Obama Raised Half a Billion Online', *The Washington Post*, available at <http://voices. washingtonpost.com/44/2008/11/20/obama_raised_half_a_billion_ on.html>, [accessed 1 October 2013].

Verbeek, Peter-Paul 2005, *What Things Do: Philosophical Reflections on Technology, Agency, and Design*, Pennsylvania University Press.

Virno, Paolo 2004, *A Grammar of the Multitude: For an Analysis of Contemporary Forms of Life*, Los Angeles, New York: Semiotex(e).

Virno, Paolo 2006, 'Reading Gilbert Simondon: Transindividuality, Technical Activity and Reification', *Radical Philosophy*, 136, March/ April, 34–43.

Wacks, Raymond 2010, *Privacy: A Very Short Introduction*, Oxford University Press 2010.

Wacks, Raymond 2013, *Privacy and Media Freedom*, Oxford University Press.

Wadsworth, Alfred P. and De Lacy Mann, Julia [1931] 1965, *The Cotton Trade and Industrial Lancashire 1600–1780*, Manchester University Press.

Weber, Max [1905] 2002, *The Protestant Ethic and the Spirit of Capitalism and Other Writings*, translated by Peter Baehr, New York, Penguin.

Weber, Samuel 2005, 'Networks, Netwars, and Narrative', in *Targets of Opportunity, On the Militarization of Thinking*, edited by Samuel Weber, Fordham University Press, 90–107.

Weiser, Mark 1991, 'The Computer for the 21st Century', *Scientific American*, 94, 94–95.

Wheeler, Michael, 2011 'Thinking Beyond the Brain: Educating and Building, from the Standpoint of Extended Cognition', *Computational Culture: A Journal of Software Studies*, 1, November, available at < http://computationalculture.net/article/beyond-the-brain>, [accessed 1 October 2013].

Wilson, Harold 1964, 'Speech Opening the Science Debate at the Party's Annual Conference, Scarbourough 1963', in *Purpose in Politics: Selected Speeches by Rt Hon Harold Wilson PC, OBE, MP*, edited by Harold Wilson, London, Weidenfeld and Nicolson, 14–28.

Winner, Langdon 1986, *The Whale and the Reactor: A Search for Limits in an Age of High Technology*, University of Chicago Press.

Žižek, Slavoj, 2010, *Living in the End Times*, London, Verso.

DOI: 10.1057/9781137373502

Web resources and apps

BishopAccountablity.org 2013, 'Documenting the Abuse Crisis in the Roman Church', available at <http://www.bishop-accountability.org/>, [accessed 1. October 2013].

Boing Boing 2013, available at <http://www.boingboing.net>, [accessed 1. October 2013]

CNN iReport 2013, available at <http://ireport.cnn.com>, [accessed 1. October 2013].

Epocrates 2013, 'Point of Care Medical Applications', available at <http://www.epocrates.com/mobile>, [accessed 1. October 2013].

Federal Election Commission 2013, 'Campaign Finance Disclosure Portal', available at <http://www.fec.gov/pindex.shtml> and <ftp://ftp.fec.gov/FEC/2008/pas208.zip>, [accessed 1. October 2013].

General Electric 2013, 'Industrial Internet', available at <http://www.ge.com/stories/industrial-internet>, [accessed 1. October 2013].

Google 2012, 'Ten Things We Know to Be True', available at <http://www.google.com/about/company/philosophy/>, [accessed 1. October 2013].

Google 2013, 'Self-Driving Car Test: Steve Mahan', available at <http://www.youtube.com/watch?v=cdgQpa1pUUE>, [accessed 1. October 2013].

IBM 2013, 'Smarter Planet', available at <http://www.ibm.com/smarterplanet/>, [accessed 1. October 2013].

NEB tools 2013, 'New England Biolabs' Most Popular Web Tools', available at <https://www.neb.com/applications>, [accessed 1 October 2013].

Opinion Space 2013, 'A Universe of Viewpoints and Ideas', available at <http://www.state.gov/opinionspace>, [accessed 1 October 2013].

The Guardian 2013, 'Investigate Your MP's Expenses', available at <http://web.archive.org/web/20120708020553/http://mps-expenses.guardian.co.uk/>, [accessed 1 October 2013].

The Lede 2013, 'Blogging the News with Robert Mackey', available at <http://thelede.blogs.nytimes.com>, [accessed 1 October 2013].

The New York Times 2011, 'The Death of a Terrorist: A Turning Point?' available at <http://www.nytimes.com/interactive/2011/05/03/us/20110503-osama-response.html>, [accessed 1 October 2013].

The New York Times Knowledge Network 2012, available at <http://www.purchase.edu/departments/academicprograms/ce/

DOI: 10.1057/9781137373502

generalinformation/noncreditcourses/nytimes.aspx>, [accessed 1 October 2013].

Sukey 2010, available at <http://www.opensukey.org>, [accessed 1 October 2013].

Swift River 2013, available at <http://www.ushahidi.com/products/swiftriver-platform>, [accessed 1 October 2013].

Ushahidi 2013, available at <http://www.ushahidi.com/>, [accessed 1 October 2013]

Ushahidi-Liberia 2013, 'Liberia Mapped', available at <http://liberia.ushahidi.com/>, [accessed 1 October 2013].

Wikileaks, available at <http://wikileaks.org>, [accessed 1 October 2013].

Films

All Watched Over by Machines of Loving Grace 2011, directed by Adam Curtis

Battleship Potemkin 1925, directed by Sergei Eisenstein

Blow Up 1966, directed by Michelangelo Antonioni

Did you know?/Shift Happens 2006, directed by Karl Fisch, Scott McLeod, available at <http://www.youtube.com/watch?v=ljbI-363A2Q>, [accessed 9 July 2012]

Dr. No 1962, directed by Terence Young

Goldfinger 1964, directed by Guy Hamilton

Inception 2011, directed by Christopher Nolan

The Spy Who Loved Me 1977, directed by Lewis Gilbert

Workers Leaving the Factory 2002 and In Comparison (Zum Verlgeich) 2009, directed by Harun Farocki

DOI: 10.1057/9781137373502

Index

DOI: 10.1057/9781137373502

DOI: 10.1057/9781137373502

DOI: 10.1057/9781137373502